A WING *and a*
PRAYER

—⁓ *A Message of Faith and Hope* ⁓—

Katharine Jefferts Schori

MOREHOUSE PUBLISHING

HARRISBURG / NEW YORK

For Dick and Keith,
who have always been willing
to share their love for high places.

Morehouse Publishing, 4775 Linglestown Road, Harrisburg, PA 17112

Morehouse Publishing, 445 Fifth Avenue, New York, NY 10016

Morehouse Publishing is an imprint of Church Publishing Incorporated.

Cover photography by Greg Preston

Cover design by Laurie Klein Westhafer

Library of Congress Cataloging-in-Publication Data

Jefferts Schori, Katharine.
  A wing and a prayer : a message of faith and hope / Katharine Jefferts Schori.
     p.   cm.
  ISBN 978-0-8192-2271-8 (pbk.)
  1. Episcopal Church—Sermons.   2. Sermons, American.   I. Title.
BX5937.J44W56   2007
252'.03—dc22

                                                        2006035168

Printed in the United States of America

07 08 09 10 11 12   10 9 8 7 6 5 4 3

Contents

Acknowledgments

I am grateful to all who have shared their passion for preaching with me over the years—most especially Linda Clader and Jude Siciliano, OP—and to those who opened the Bible to me in new ways, particularly Mary Timothy McHatten, OP, and Marcus Borg. I give thanks for those who taught me to see the world in all its created glory, especially Mary Rose Neff, Chuck Baxter, Don Abbott, Isabella Abbott, Jim McCauley, and Bill Pearcy.

Wild Blue Yonder...

Flying reminds me that the word we translate "spirit" means several things—wind, breath, and spirit, whether we're talking about the Hebrew of the Old Testament or the Greek of the New.

Sometimes it's a headwind, slowing us down until we feel like we're hardly moving.

Sometimes it's a gloriously fast tailwind, speeding us on our way.

Sometimes it's just downright bumpy, like coming into the airport on a hot afternoon—and maybe enough to make us a bit airsick . . .

And sometimes, when you're downstream from one of these big mountain ranges on a good windy day, it's even like surfing.

Life is like that—the wind and the spirit blow where they will, and we rarely know the direction, or how the wind will carry us, until we're in the midst of it.

Yet that wind and breath and spirit help us do things we couldn't or wouldn't do alone.

Flying depends both on the physical wind and on the inventive spirit that led the Wright brothers and others to figure out how to harness that wind. And in the early Church, those folks we read about in Acts began to speak not only in other languages, but boldly, so much so that the onlookers thought they were drunk. They began to tell good news to people who weren't sure what it meant at first.

Sometimes that wind/breath/spirit moves us to bring comfort in the face of death and destruction—whether it's to the people trying to live after an earthquake in Java, or to the friends and family of a child killed by violence. The newspaper on any given day has stories about children who die of abuse in America, who suffer from AIDS in India. How will the spirit move *us* to respond?

The spirit of God is also called "paraclete" and "comforter." *Paraclete* is the Greek word for a supporter who will come and stand alongside—somebody you can call on in time of need. And *comforter* means more than a cozy old quilt. Literally, it means "to strengthen much." This spirit emboldens; it brings solace and strength. When we gather together to worship, we say that we come to the table "not for solace only, but for strength." That is the comforting spirit.

The spirit is also life-giving breath, the energy that literally drives our respiration, our breathing in and breathing out. Life soon flees without it. How does the spirit bring new life to us? What is the energy that keeps our communities lively and growing?

Newness and growth are part of what it means to live in God, and as those disciples were visited by a rushing wind, and tongues of fire, and filled with spirit, they became more than they were before, both new creatures and a new community. There is a wonderful reprise here of the first creation story in Genesis, when a wind from God (or the breath or spirit of God) moved over the chaotic waters at the beginning of creation. And we're blessed with new beginnings, all the time. That's what being open to the spirit is about.

We're all afloat in a sky or sea of spirit, even though we have different experiences of it. We're always surrounded by the reality of the spirit, even when we don't realize or recognize it. There are occasions like Pentecost that bring great in-breakings of awareness, and there are other, smaller, daily miracles of re-creation—like the kindness of a stranger urging us to go first, or the assurance of a friend that we are being remembered in prayer, or the guileless smile of a toddler, or the hand we hold in a hospice room.

There's a great and ancient tradition in the icons of the orthodox branch of the Church, an icon that shows the disciples gathered around a room, each one with a little flaming tongue. Each disciple is significantly different—each has different clothes, each is a different color, each looks in a different direction, and each has a unique face. Like the ability to hear in our own languages, we too are blessed with many gifts, but one spirit. There is a figure at the bottom of that icon called Cosmos—all creation—

who holds many scrolls, each meant to represent the truth that will deliver us from darkness. The striking thing is that there isn't just one scroll. Each human being gets his or her own scroll, and each speaks of truth. Each one has access to that truth, but only God contains the fullness of truth. The spirit speaks to us all, and it is in the community, in the Body of Christ, that we can approach that fullness of truth—no single individual has it all. And perhaps that truth cannot be fully known in space and time, but only in eternity. The spirit helps us do and discover things we haven't the strength to do alone.

The General Convention—that once-every-three-years meeting of the Episcopal Church—had the potential to be a Pentecost event. Not only were there Episcopalians in attendance from the United States and Haiti and Taiwan and Honduras, but worship celebrations in many heritages—French and Spanish as well as English, but also in Creole, Lakota, Taiwanese, German, Italian, Navajo, Swahili, and other languages. We experienced different traditions of singing, dance, prayer, praise, and preaching. We heard different opinions and experiences as we gathered around our tables every day to reflect on the Bible. And we tried to hear the spirit speaking in every person who gathered to debate the many resolutions we considered. We had many experiences of the spirit—some felt like battling a headwind, some like afternoon turbulence, and some like a mighty tailwind.

Our task, and the task of every community of the spirit, is openness and eagerness to receive spirit, whether it feels like surfing or battling upwind. Our task is a willingness to be surprised, an openness to those accusations of drunkenness—being drunk on God, which is what enthusiasm means. Our task is to be open to being changed, and being re-created, and being filled with boldness. Our task is to be willing to partner with this inspired community to change the world.

We don't know what God will do in our communities and in our world, but the inspired thing will have something to do with bringing peace and strength, with re-creating our church as a community where no child is abused and no parent ever reaches that point of despair. Our task is to keep listening and responding.

The essays that follow started out as sermons—my own attempt to boldly proclaim the ways I've seen the spirit moving in communities as diverse as those on the coast of Oregon and the deserts of the Southwest and the mountain ranges of the Appalachians. The essays look at my dream for the Church and the reckless, abundant love of the God we serve. That's the dream that I bring to the Episcopal Church as I serve as presiding bishop.

Breathe deeply, know the wind of God is always beneath your wings, receive holy spirit, and change the world.

PART ONE

BODY-BUILDING
Nurturing the Body of Christ

One Body,
Many Members

I spend a lot of time on airplanes, and I'm struck by how many different people are needed to put one of those big planes in the air. Think about the journey from beginning to end. We encounter ticket agents and reservations people, either the ones at our local travel agent or the folks who write the Internet programs, as well as the folks who check us in at the airport. There are the people who design the ticket forms and figure out how to price the seats—and we all know that travelers probably pay thirteen different prices for the same trip. There are baggage handlers: at the curb, in the terminal, and the ones we never see who load the bags into the cargo hold. There are scores of mechanics working to keep planes flying safely. What about the people who clean the airplane, so we don't have to sit in a seat full of somebody else's banana peels and old newspapers? There are kitchen workers, menu planners, the farmers who grow the food that's served, people who run the factories that put soda and juice in cans, and truck drivers and delivery people who get all that stuff to the right airplane at the right time.

And then there are the people we are used to seeing—the flight attendants, pilots, and navigators. If you take a window seat you may be aware of some of the ground crew—the folks who direct traffic on the ground with flags and lights, showing the pilot which gate to enter, or the flight controllers in the tower.

There are some other people we rarely think about—the FAA inspectors who keep flying safer than driving to the airport; the legislators who help to ensure that the system has oversight and funding; and then the people who run the airlines—managers, CEOs, the investors who fund the purchase of new aircraft, and the other passengers who help to provide a market. After all, those planes don't fly just for us!

Think of even deeper levels: the titanium miners and aluminum smelters and petroleum refiners and construction engineers, even interior decorators. Somebody designed those little reading lights that never seem to shine in the right place to light your book. What about the utility workers who provide the water and energy to run all the networks and systems that it takes to go from the first conception of a new airplane to getting that bird into the sky? Every single one of them is an essential part of our hop from Portland or Eugene to Denver or New York or Tokyo.

Scientists are teaching us that everything in the universe is connected, not just complex human and mechanical systems. A remarkable experiment a number of years ago showed this in a new way. If you take a pair of electrons with opposite spins, and send them off in different directions, and then change the spin of one of them, the spin of the other also changes—instantaneously. We're beginning to understand that everything in the universe is connected, even at the most elemental level.

We've begun to see this on a global scale as we notice that the average temperature is going up and the weather is changing—here, in Australia, and in northern Europe. The permafrost in the Yukon is melting. Sea level is gradually increasing as the ice cover at the poles begins to melt faster than it's deposited as snow. Islands in the South Pacific are slowly disappearing—some inhabited islands will be under water before too many more decades go by if the global climate change continues.

Paul makes this point emphatically when he says that the Body of Christ has lots of different parts, all vital to the health of the body. Which part is extraneous? Can we do without the foot, or the ear, or the eye? We are the Body of Christ—is there anybody here we don't need? Anyone we can do without? Who's extraneous?

The world is inclined to say that we don't need the homeless, or immigrants, or people of different ethnic backgrounds. Until fairly recently our society ignored handicapped people and the mentally ill—we shut them away so we wouldn't have to see and live with them. But Jesus speaks to those very people in the synagogue—the blind, the poor, and those in prison. They are the ones he honors.

What is it about human nature that wants to ignore some kinds of people?

What or who tells us we don't need those people? I don't know about your experience, but I've been in some environments where that kind of thinking comes pretty easily. The cattle car called a commercial airplane is one of them. I don't want to be connected at the elbow or hip to the person in the next seat. I don't want to hear the crying baby in the next row all the way across the country. I don't want to stand in line for what feels like hours until they call my row for boarding. I don't want to remember that all of the folks crowding into the airport are part of the system that makes air travel affordable and relatively convenient. What do all these strangers have to do with me? But I need every single one of them, even and maybe especially when I find that hard to remember.

Each one of us is connected to the people enduring civil war in the Congo, Sudan, and the Holy Land, to the victims of earthquake in El Salvador, to the homeless individuals and families along the railroad tracks and under the bridges of Corvallis and New York. There is no one that "we have no need of."

When Jesus stood in that synagogue and read words of hope and deliverance, he inaugurated a new government—a government of and by and for those whom others think disposable. This reign of God is a way of living that is most concerned with the poor, the captives, the blind, and the oppressed. They get top priority.

Our role in government, too, begins with our neighbor. Our task as citizens of the the world and of the reign of God is to keep asking, "Who is the focus of this earthly government? Who receives the greatest concern— those who are poor, or those who have never been poor? Those in prison or those who have never been in prison?"

The governing principles of God's reign aren't designed to make any of us particularly comfortable. When we think about the poor, captives, blind, and oppressed, do we know they have need of us? All are members of the body of God's creation, all have need of one another. Sometimes even those occasions when we feel most cut off can be reminders of our connectedness. A few years ago I sat on a small plane going from Miami to Orlando, behind a woman of about forty and a little girl of about two. As their story unfolded during the journey, I learned that this beautiful child was coming from Central America with her adoptive mother-to-be. The woman's husband and older daughter were waiting in Orlando to meet the newest member of their family. The world grew smaller and connections came closer in that act of deliverance. An orphan found a home, and a captive was set free to discover the riches of a family's love. It was an act of love that didn't make any economic sense. It was an act that noticed and cherished one of the least of God's creatures in this hemisphere.

Is there anyone we feel we have no need of? A good spiritual exercise might be to figure out where and how we can reach out to someone we would rather ignore. Each of those acts inaugurates the reign of God yet again. Every one of those acts can proclaim, as Jesus did, "Today, this scripture is fulfilled in your hearing." Today we are sent to bring good news to the poor, to release the captives, to heal the blind, to let the oppressed go free, so that together we may proclaim the year of God's favor.

Tending the Wounded Body of Christ

Let's think about where we've come from. Each one of us is the product of a long line of parents, grandparents, and even more distant ancestors—all of them people who have had something important to pass along to us, including love, and faith, and hope.

We live in an age when there doesn't seem to be a great deal of hope. Maybe you read in the paper a while back about the giant dust cloud that astronomers believe the Earth is going to run into in twenty thousand years or so. What was your reaction? I know there was a piece of me that said, "Oh well, in twenty thousand years there probably won't be any intelligent life left on this planet, so what does it matter?" Well, a lot of the young people in this country see drive-by shootings next door, and no meaningful employment in their neighborhoods, and it affects their lives today and tomorrow, not thousands of years from now. And we wonder why those kids don't have any hope. Toni Morrison put it this way in a speech: "The course of time seems to be narrowing to a vanishing point beyond which humanity neither exists nor wants to. It is singular, this diminished, already withered desire for a future." Hopelessness seems to be the leprosy of our day. And it's a disease that's infected much of a generation.

Where did our hope for a future come from? Where did we learn to trust that we'll wake up tomorrow morning? Why do we believe that there's a reason to make plans, to aim at something better? It's got something to do with that bit in Exodus about Israel being God's treasured possession. God is telling Israel: "I love you, I care about you, I rescued you from those slavers in Egypt, and I carried you like a mother eagle cares for her baby eaglets, prompting them to fly, even pushing them from the nest, but always there under their wings with reassurance when it's needed. You have to know that you are valued because of the care I have shown you.

And now you motley crew are going to be a nation of priests, so you can show the rest of the world what I mean."

None of this makes any sense at all, at least from the standpoint of logic. It's sort of like the class klutz being chosen captain of the softball team. Israel isn't anything to write home about—they're a bunch of whiners, and they run away the first chance they get. They're just like us. But God tells them they're going to be the star players—like Moses, the fellow with a speech impediment, who gets the lead in the drama. If you think about it, the same thing happens in the gospel. Jesus asks all these ordinary folks to come and follow him—they're a bunch of nobodies in the world's terms—fishers and tax collectors . . . and grocery clerks and accountants and loggers and engineers. And all those nobody Israelites and nobody apostles hear that they're God's special possession, and by God, they begin to believe it. And the world changes—because they know they *are* somebody. Peter and all the rest of them struggle with it, and they still have their doubts, just like Moses, but look at what was wrought through them.

Jesus tells his band of special nobodies that the harvest is plentiful—there are lives waiting to be changed out there, but there aren't so many laborers just yet—those blessed nobodies who say yes to that hopeful message—the ones who have heard that they are God's special possession. Think for a minute what it means to be a treasure—it's something rare, of great value, something that's preserved at all costs. Something precious, like diamonds or gold or a rare flower or a warm, sunny day in January. Moses gets to tell all Israel that they are God's treasure. And then Israel gets to tell the rest of the world.

I used to teach a class on world religions at Oregon State University. I learned an awful lot, and not that much of it had to do with different religious traditions. The students in my class were fairly representative of what's often called Generation X. I don't think there was one over thirty, and there was some mix of religious background in the class, from Hindu and Buddhist and Muslim to several different kinds of Christian. But probably 10 or 15 percent of the class had absolutely no religious background at all. Zip. Nada. Nothing. But most of them were in the class because they were looking for something.

One of the requirements of the course was to visit four different religious services, Christian and non-Christian. They had to turn in a report that said something about what they experienced, and what they learned from talking to the worshippers. Many of the students went with great trepidation, and some of them found the experience as a whole quite challenging, particularly the ones who went to Buddhist meditation groups—sitting in silence for thirty minutes to an hour at a time is not easy.

What struck me over and over, however, were the reactions they elicited when they asked questions, and the care with which they were treated. One student wanted to visit a Bahai worship group, and was told that inquirers had to go to an information session first. When he told them it was for a class, they relented and welcomed him into their home with great warmth.

One woman in the class called a mosque asking about services, and told the man who took her call that she was visiting for a class. He not only met her in the parking lot when she arrived, but arranged for a Muslim woman to be there to answer her questions. Students were warmly welcomed into Orthodox Jewish services, a Buddhist temple in Portland, and various Christian churches up and down the Willamette Valley. There were a few uncomfortable experiences, usually when students felt they were being told "What we do is the only right way, and you're doomed if you don't join us." The students were very quick to recognize when members of the various religious communities were interested in them only as potential converts, or as a means to an end—a way to improve their numbers. Many of the students finished the term with a vision of what belonging to a religious community can mean—even the ones with no religious background. Many came away from their experience feeling valued as a human being, which they often reported with surprise. This doesn't seem to be a normative experience in their lives.

Many of these students had the experience of being treated as God's special possession. They were shown what it means to be treasured. It doesn't take a great deal—it's mostly an attitude of hospitality, of warmth and openness and caring. It means relating to someone as though he or she were infinitely valuable. And, wonder of wonders, it leads to hopefulness.

This kind of caring is an important part of what it means to be a nation of priests, and to proclaim the good news that the kingdom has come near. We might use that as shorthand for the kingdom of God—when every person is valued for the infinite treasure she or he is.

As members of the Body of Christ, we can cure the sickness that is hopelessness. We can wash away the leprosy of listlessness. We can cast out the demon of despair. We have received God's love without payment, we can give without payment. We can show what it means to be treasured. We all get opportunities like these to be priests—we can show others that they too are God's special possession. And those opportunities don't come primarily at church. Whether we have descendants or not, all of us can act as parents, mentors, teachers, and gospellers. We meet treasures everywhere we go. We can offer a sense of what it means to be treasured. We can offer hope in every encounter. And that's the richest and most fruitful kind of gospelling there is.

Collective Memory

I went flying yesterday morning—both for a bit of a lark and to keep the engine lubricated, because I hadn't run it for three weeks. My husband and I flew from Las Vegas over to Shoshone, California, where I'd heard there was a place to get breakfast right by the airport. We found the tiny little airstrip, and walked across the street to a café. It was a place out of time—the tables were covered with Indian prints like the ones so popular in the 1970s, there was lots of wonderful art on the walls, and all sorts of books scattered about—Rumi's poetry, books on the desert, comparative religion, and on and on. There was one other customer, and before too long we all struck up a conversation. The other customer comes to Shoshone every year for a time away—something he needs as a divorce lawyer in Los Angeles. The owner of the restaurant is a forty-something Las Vegas native who's enjoying making gourmet food and living *way* out in the desert.

It was a remarkable experience of discovery and, in an odd way, remembering. That word, "remember," often seems to be just about recovering bits of data in our memory banks. But it has a far richer constellation of meaning for Christians. When Jesus says, "Do this in remembrance of me"—and when we say that in the middle of communion—we not only bring to mind Jesus and his life, death, and resurrection, but we also bring together the various parts of Christ's body. We gather the members into one. Something like that happened over coffee in that café so aptly named "C'est si bon." It is so good! It was not quite déjà vu, but it was the remembering of a body previously unknown.

When the thief being crucified with Jesus asks him to "remember me when you come into your kingdom," Jesus responds, "You will be with me today in paradise." That's not just later, when they're both dead and gone, but right now. Jesus' kingdom, Jesus' reign of peace and shalom, isn't just far off. It is right here and right now, if we want to look for it, if we are willing to remember.

We surely live in that peaceable kingdom when we gather around the communion table, even and especially with folks who challenge us, disappoint us, frustrate us, or have wronged us. The table is a sign that communion with God is possible for thieves and criminals, for people who are significant pains in the neck, and for every one of us. The table is the concrete possibility of communion with God in those previously unknown.

Think about other tables we gather around for holidays or family events. Our table traditions say something about our ways of gathering and re-membering. Close your eyes and think about who is there at your table. Aunt Mary the drama queen, Uncle John who always comes half-soused and will be downright obnoxious before the day is over, the cousins who differ loudly about every issue in politics, Granny the family gossip, and the variously wild, sanctimonious, or downright mischievous children underfoot. That's not a bad image for the church and for the kingdom of God—the scratchy proximity of near enemies, who come together because deep down, under all those more or less functional facades, they really do love each other.

As we gather around our tables, we also call to mind those who are not with us: those who have joined the communion of saints, those absent because they have been called to duty in Iraq, Afghanistan, or somewhere else across the globe. We call to mind those who are absent because their relationship with the rest of the body is torn or fractured. When you gather around your family table, remember those who are present and those who are absent. Remember those who have no access to a table of plenty. Our remembering can be a vision of God's kingdom, and a way for us to begin to make it real.

That good thief who asks to be remembered is told that today he will be in paradise. Most of us hear that simply as another word for heaven. It's got a richer history, though. The word "paradise" comes from the Middle Eastern word for a walled garden. It's got something in common with many fenced-in backyards—a place of safety, an oasis in the midst of the desert, where life is protected and flourishing—and it certainly echoes the Garden of Eden, surrounded and walled in by those four rivers of plenty. It also has something in common with "this fragile earth, our island home" as one of our prayers puts it. There is a clear implication that this walled garden includes us all—even that other criminal hanging next to Jesus, whose response is not repentance but mockery. The only difference between those two thieves—and those who find themselves in paradise and those who don't—is whether or not they've awakened to the possibility. It is not, however, simply a matter of putting on some rose-colored glasses.

The remembering that brings us into paradise is both about bringing to mind what we've already known or experienced, and about a dream for the future, for what is possible in God's creation. Remembering is about the truths of our faith as well as the possibilities for making those truths real now and in the future.

I heard a different version of the traditional Thanksgiving story. Robert Two Bulls is Lakota and a priest of the Diocese of Los Angeles who has written about our fond myths of the first Thanksgiving. We remember, and we teach our children about, the Pilgrims, who came to these shores seeking religious freedom. Most of them came because they felt oppressed by the Church of England, the church that gave life to the Episcopal Church in the United States. Once they got here, those Pilgrims were not as free as we recall. Their search for religious freedom did not include religious freedom for those who disagreed with them. But they have continued to have a significant influence on the cultural underpinnings of this land as we see in local and national elections.

We remember the works of those early settlers as largely beneficent— settling an empty land, growing crops, and filling the land with their descendants. In reality, they unwittingly spread disease that killed off many of the native people, enslaved many of those who were left, and stole their land. By and large, they did not do any of those things with utterly evil intent. But the results were not something for which it is easy to give thanks.

The first Thanksgiving is recalled as a gracious meal shared by European settlers and the native people who had taught the settlers how to survive in a strange land. The Wampanoag Indian who played a large part in that story was named Squanto or Tisquantum. He did teach the Pilgrims how to grow crops and how to survive on foreign soil. He already spoke English when they arrived, because he had been taken to England by earlier settlers, and kept there for years as a slave. When he finally came home, 90 percent of the people in his village were gone, victims of smallpox. In spite of his history, or perhaps because of it, Squanto "remembered" a vision of peoples settled together in peace. He did not remember a body of people who were out to oppress him and his people.

That vision of peoples settled together in peace has a great deal to do with the paradise of which Jesus speaks. We are all in the same walled garden—Americans, Iraqis, North Koreans, and the French. Whether or not it is paradise depends on what and who we remember.

What will you remember around your family table? What will that vision do for those who gather? And for those who are absent? What dream are you remembering?

You Can't Always Get
What You Want

At the 2000 General Convention of the Episcopal Church the budget presentation began with loud rock music: "You can't always get what you want ..." (The Rolling Stones). You can't always get what you want, but if you try sometime, you just might find you get what you need.

That's a pretty fair statement of the gospel story of the laborers in the vineyard. Those workers all got a day's wage, which is what they needed. All of them went to the marketplace that morning needing a job for the day, and ready to work for it. The complaining Israelites got what they needed in the wilderness, no more and no less. It's an interesting message—maybe whining works, and daily bread is provided simply because it is needed, and it doesn't depend on how hard you work or how long you wait to start working.

Oh, does that offend our capitalist hearts! And our Puritan work ethic! And all our systems of behavior management that reward the desired behavior and punish the undesired. God's justice and God's mercy don't look like ours.

Most of us, most of the time, expect things to be fair. And our sense of fairness assumes a predictable and fundamental relationship between behavior and outcome.

But it looks as though the only behavior that's necessary to receive blessing is being in need, or maybe just recognizing that you are in need. The winery workers went to the market because they needed a job so they could eat. The Israelites were hungry. But the degree of blessing doesn't seem to depend on desire or earnestness of prayer or length of labor. Everybody gets the same, and it's enough and plenty.

That radical equality offends us because most of us believe, somewhere deep down, that we deserve what we have, that we've done something right to be as blessed as we are. And the parable of the winery workers and the story of Exodus seem to tell us that however hard we work, it doesn't matter. We will receive enough, just what we need, our daily bread.

Maybe it's a bit easier if we think about the gifts we have. What are you good at, what are your particular and unique talents? If we look around, sometimes we're tempted to put a higher value on particular gifts—either ours seem especially valuable, or somebody else's seem to be worth far more than our own. But each one of us—each member of the Body of Christ—has what we need to grow into the full stature of Christ, into the beloved human being we were created to be. We've got enough—whether it's a good head for numbers, or a soft heart for children, or a wide streak of risk-taking. The color of our skin, our bodily limitation or ability, our intellectual and emotional capacity—all the givenness of our creation, are just that—gifts that are blessing enough. That doesn't mean that we can't do heroic things with those gifts, but heroism or distinction is infinitely variable—it depends only on what we do with what we have.

Those laborers who spent almost all day waiting in the marketplace had a heroic kind of faith. They could have gone home in the middle of the day, for it was pretty unlikely that anyone was going to come along and hire them. They continued to hope for what was needed, and they found it.

Years ago, I was given a two-week trip to Turkey and Israel. I didn't ask for it, I didn't deserve it, I didn't pay for it. It just appeared; it was purely a gift. In Turkey, we traveled around to see many of the churches that Paul names in his letters. But over and over again, I saw something really odd—in markets, in restaurants, and hotels—little blue things that looked sort of like eyes. The guide finally told us that they were supposed to be a protection against the evil eye. I think most of us simply dismissed them as a local superstition. When we got to Israel, we saw just as many, and I must admit I was puzzled to see these amulets in shops right alongside the crosses and stars of David.

Remember what the vineyard owner says to the all-day workers who complain about their wages? "Can't I do what I choose with what belongs to me? Or are you envious because I am generous?" In Greek, the last part literally says, "Do you have the evil eye because I am good?" Those little blue eyes we saw all over the Middle East were meant to remind people about the evil that comes from looking with an envious eye.

How do we look at other people's blessings? Do we get angry because it seems like someone else has more? A God's-eye view doesn't see scarcity— it's all abundance. Everybody gets what is needed in the kingdom of God. God is more like a Jewish or Italian mother who urges us to "eat, eat, people will think I don't love you if you're too skinny!" There is daily bread for all in God's vineyard.

Think for a minute how different the world would look if we saw abundantly. Maybe rather than asking, "Give us today our daily bread," we'd give thanks for the daily bread we have already received. That kind of an understanding seems a lot more in line with what Jesus says about the lilies of the field, and don't worry about what you're going to eat or wear, and the traditional Jewish blessing that goes, "Blessed are you, Lord God of the universe, for you give us bread from the earth." I've seen that intrinsic attitude of abundance most directly among the ordinary people of Mexico and recent immigrants in this country. There is a cultural expectation that sees blessing in what is, and if it is a blessing, then it is certainly more than enough and should be shared. On All Souls' Day in Mexico, families celebrate the lives of their loved ones who have died in the last year by holding an open house. Everybody in town is invited—friends, neighbors, strangers, and even tourists. For hours, people file through the house, offering prayers for the deceased and paying respects to the family. And every single person is fed and given something to drink. It is a celebration that says "God has blessed us in the person who died, and so we will share our blessing with the world."

Blessed are you, God of the universe, for the abundance you have showered on each of us. It is enough, and more than enough. Make our hearts glad, open our hands, and let us see through eyes of blessing.

Total Ministry

Ministry grows out of the Body of Christ. We may not agree on the language to use in talking about that ministry—we hear terms like total ministry, mutual ministry, and ministry of all the baptized, but all ministry is grounded in baptism. If it's going to be effective ministry, it has to recognize the connectedness of that Body, and express that awareness in collaboration.

The ministry we received at baptism calls us to transform our communities into something that looks more like the reign of God. That is our mission, and it has shaped the way we understand what it means to be the Church. In other words, that way of seeing ourselves as the Body of Christ is based in a specific ecclesiology.

In my travels around the church, I've been repeatedly struck by the fears and resistance that arise when total ministry comes up. What is it that so threatens people when we begin to talk about gifted baptismal ministers and ministries? When we insist that ministry is a mark of the Body of Christ, rather than the right or possession of an individual?

I am certain that some of those fears have to do with a perceived threat to professional clergy. I've heard those fears: "What will happen to my job and my livelihood?" Sometimes it's even deeper: "What will happen to my position? My authority?" And from congregations: "If the priest is no longer the resident expert with all the answers, how will we survive? Where will we look for answers or direction?"

I am convinced that we will need all the seminary graduates we can produce in the coming years. But they will need to be formed and deployed differently. In the West, especially the rural West, we will desperately need well-educated ministry developers. We need people who can invite others into ministry as equippers and collaborators. But the reality also is that most small rural parishes cannot provide either financial or ministerial rewards adequate to employ such a highly trained professional. There is simply not enough "church work" to fill forty hours a week in tiny congregations. However, there are lots of opportunities for the Episcopalians in those communities to use their gifts in baptismal ministry 24/7, and the church's role is to continue to equip and support those daily ministries. A priest is needed at most a few hours a week. There's probably more work for a deacon, but not all parishes have a deacon.

This is a resource issue. To form and educate a "professional" cleric takes a hundred thousand dollars and a three-year displacement, often from family and usually from livelihood. To invest those kinds of resources in someone who will serve a congregation of twelve people seems, at the very least, wasteful. Small, remote congregations do need someone with those gifts, but they may need to be shared with other communities.

The other fear about this ecclesiology has to do with the underlying expectation that the baptized will take up their ministerial crosses daily and grow up into the full stature of Christ. The reality is that the Church has long been in the business of engendering dependence, and that clearly does not lead to full baptismal ministry!

We need leaders in the church—and I insist that every baptized person is a Christian leader somewhere—who know how to lay down their lives for others. We need leaders who are engaged in daily ministry in the world, we need ordained leaders, and we need those who blur the boundaries.

We don't need prima donnas, who need to be the center of ecclesiastical attention. The last time I checked, the Body of Christ already had a head, and it's not you or me or the rector down the street.

Nor do we need passive consumers of ministry who refuse to be adults in this Body. Being children of God does not mean being childish.

We need people who know how to give themselves and their ministries away. There's an old theological term, *kenosis*, that means emptying. It's most often used in reference to God becoming human. If we are made in the image of God, it should characterize our being as well. Our ministry needs to be kenotic. The ordained are called to be icons, models, but not the primary doers of ministry! Our job is to equip the saints, to provide formation, education, guidance, support, and then to get out of the way. Sometimes it means leaving a hole, an opening for another to serve.

Consider St. Alban, the first martyr in Britain, who around the year 304 laid down his life for a friend. His martyrdom was baptismal ministry. It was not the priest who was martyred, but the newly baptized, the one washed so clean his name becomes a symbol of his baptism, the one whose family and race is Christian. There's a wonderful question in Alban's story.

Where was the priest? Was he hiding, or was he getting out of the way so Alban could make his witness?

Our ministry together in Nevada (while I speak of Nevada's experience here, I believe this is common to all dioceses and all judicatories) has included weathering the usual crises. All of them, without exception, were about the abuse of authority and position, either by clergy or parish officers. We've dealt with child abuse and sexual exploitation, we've seen one person exploit a parish by retiring in place to satisfy that cleric's financial needs. We've seen clergy and vestry officers misuse and steal parish funds—usually because of gambling addictions. We've had both clergy and lay leaders bully others in order to get their way. We've seen other leaders manipulate almost everything to focus on themselves. Universally, these crises are precipitated by narcissism, egotism, self-centeredness, or in our technical terms, idolatry—and sin. They're initiated by people who cannot, will not, or do not know how to lay down their lives for others. And believe me, it's equal opportunity—it occurs among the ordained, both locally and seminary-trained, and lay leaders.

Laying down one's life for others usually begins in letting go of our fond prejudices, and letting God surprise us. It means looking beyond our own narrow desires or ancient expectations. Dying to self is both the crux of ministry and the cross. There is no other way to the reign of God.

A baptismal ecclesiology begins in the belief that every member of this church is gifted for, and called to, ministry. It asserts that no ministry is more important than another, but that all are equally valued expressions of members of the Body of Christ. And this ecclesiology announces that the reign of God is our end. We go toward it as we lay down our lives for the rest of what Sallie McFague,[1] an ecological theologian and author, calls the Body of God—those in the church and those beyond it, humanity and the rest of creation.

As leaders in this Body, our job is to welcome the prophet, the one who speaks for God rather than self. Our job is to equip those around us to see beyond their own needs and wants. Our job is to model that kind of sacrificial living. That is baptismal ministry and it is the foundation of ordained ministry.

Lay down your life and receive it back a thousand-fold.

---

1. Sally McFague is the author of *Metaphorical Theology* (Minneapolis: Augsburg Fortress, 1997) and *The Body of God* (Minneapolis: Augsburg Fortress, 1993).

Saints in Our Midst

Gather for me seventy of the elders of Israel, whom you know to be the priests of the people and rectors over them, bring them to the house of the Lord, and have them take their place in the Councils of the Church (cf. Num 11:16).

We'd write it down a bit differently today—bring me those who are spiritual elders, the pastors and spiritual leaders among them . . . and seventy still wouldn't be enough.

But there are those who grumble, and diminish the calling of those who never went to the tent of meeting or a seminary. But there are plenty of prophets out there, and they're busy speaking for the Lord. They are busy prophesying in the various camps where they live and work. And God is still bringing unexpected gifts and surprises. Consider the retired physics professor who started a prison congregation; the AIDS educator who works incessantly for awareness in black communities; the priest-activist who labors on behalf of the homeless and against nuclear weapons and is learning Spanish to better serve his parishioners.

Each of these people was called, trained, and each also serves a more or less "normal" Sunday congregation. They, and many others, have vital and creative ministries in congregations as well as in the world. They serve in an incredible variety of ways: as newspaper publishers, nurses, as scientists and teachers, in public relations and in sales, as photographers, county recorders, prison guards, school janitors, park rangers, booksellers, museum curators, and as chaplains in hospitals, hospices, prisons, and jails. Each one speaks for God in the camp where he or she labors, as well as in the Sunday tent of meeting.

But there are also lay people who live their faith in baptismal ministry every day of their lives. The great gift of the ministry of all the baptized is just that—it's a re-membering of Christ's ministering body. When each one of us was baptized, we were called into ministry. We are only just beginning to live into this theology. The saints in our midst are not unlike the saints in the places where you serve—they are heroes and witnesses and builders of the reign of God. Consider the two retired educators who publish a monthly news article addressing issues of social justice; the aviation inspector who works to build a new Hispanic congregation in his area; the lawyer who provides free legal help to those unable to pay.

If all those stories are not surprise enough, what about your own? Did you leave the womb, or the family home, expecting to go where you are today? What odd places has God asked you to visit? What strange and wonderful ministries have beckoned you?

Would that all God's people were prophets, and that the Lord would put the Spirit on each one of them!

Who's Got a
Hold on You?

Episcopalians and Lutherans may be bound together by a common Eucharist, and a common ministry, but we still have lots of things to learn about one another.

Dear Mr. Keillor,

I've been wondering if you picture the Lake Wobegon Lutherans as ELCA Lutherans. If so, what do you think of the new communion between the Lutheran and Episcopal churches, and thus what would the good reserved Scandinavian folks there in Minnesota think of their more liberal Anglican brethren?

Aidan[2]

Humorist and author Garrison Keillor points to cultural differences and how we react to the people around us who bring a different experience. Those differences are a mission opportunity, and an opening to share the reality of God's love. Together, Lutherans and Episcopalians are focusing on that mission, particularly with the unchurched and with those whose mother tongue is Spanish.

When mission comes up, think about that old TV show *Mission: Impossible*. Peter Graves gets an invitation from a mysterious Secretary, and if he accepts it, off he goes to save the world in fifty-nine minutes. We're charged with a mission too, even if our time frame is a bit longer—or shorter.

We get our invitation first at baptism, when we are claimed for God's mission: to build the reign of God on earth by sharing the love of God in Christ. That word "claim" comes from a word that means to cry out or call—it's about vocation, and it's about hearing with compassion. There's

---

2. Personal correspondence from the Very Rev. Don Brown, Dean of the Cathedral, Sacramento, retired.

some old gospel language that talks about this claim as "he's got a hold on me."

Now—where or how have you been claimed? Who's got a hold on you?

I recently visited a parish for confirmation. During my homily I noticed a street person over on one side of the church, and during the peace, a couple in the back went over to him and welcomed him. The man came up for communion, the last in line, with some real wariness in his eyes, no shoes on his feet, and with dirt ground deep into his hands. I shared bread with him, but he left without taking the wine. As the service finished, he went out the side door without speaking to anyone. I had an appointment with a member of the congregation afterward, and we decided to walk along the river. We walked out of the church building down to the river, and here was the man who'd been in church, with two bicycle cops putting him in handcuffs. And the best I could do was say, "We'll pray for you." He's got a hold on me.

On Tuesdays the secretary in the diocesan office goes home at noon. If I hear the phone, I answer it. I've had some very interesting calls, sometimes asking for the nearest church, sometimes for financial assistance. One Tuesday, a woman called and told me about seeing her spirits rising in front of her. My initial conclusion was "mentally ill." But as she went on, she began to tell me that she was possessed. And I began to wonder, "Is she on drugs?" She denied it repeatedly as she went on with her story. And at the last, what I could do was to offer to pray with her and call a priest I know who understands the Afro-Caribbean religious culture and also has good social work skills. She's got a hold on me.

A few days later I was stopped at a red light and saw a man in the median up ahead of me with a cardboard sign asking for money. And then suddenly he was scooting across the street. I looked around to find out why, and saw a cop running after him. Our streets have to be clean, you see, because we depend so much on tourists. He's got a hold on me.

Yesterday the pastor of our African Christian Fellowship came to see me. He and most of the congregation are immigrants from Kenya and other parts of East Africa. He had good news—his family are well, and his work is going well—and bad news—two of the members of his congregation are in jail with immigration problems. I could offer the name of one of our deacons, who is the prison chaplain. She can get Fr. Kasio in to see Mr. Kagombe and Mr. Kamau. They have a hold on me.

Who's got a hold on you? Who has a claim on you? Whose cries do you hear?

Jesus, on the road again, "had to go through Samaria."

It sounds a good deal like saying he had to drive through Watts, or Harlem, or North Las Vegas. Jesus' people felt the same way about Samaria as many Americans do about the ghettos and barrios around us. But Jesus walks in and parks himself right by the water fountain in the middle of town. In the heat of the day, all the decent folk are home taking a siesta. But when this nameless woman of questionable reputation turns up, Jesus talks with her longer than anyone else in the gospels. Jesus cries out to her for water—he has a hold on her—and as they debate, it turns out that she has a hold on Jesus— he offers her a different kind of water and invites her into a new kind of relationship.

In a place like Las Vegas, the midday sun and cries for water have just as immediate an import. Noel Coward's observation that "only mad dogs and Englishmen go out in the noonday sun" doesn't hold around here. The heat of summer sees our streets filled with the homeless, the mentally ill, and sunburned tourists with too much flesh, too few clothes, and too little sense/cents. Our construction industry is among the fastest growing in the country, and the worksites are often populated by immigrants who may have no words to ask for water, or expectations of justice that will allow them time to drink it. They are all thirsty for water that satisfies— for water that will slake their dryness, and for justice that will pour down like an ever-flowing stream.

Who has a hold on you? Who has laid claim to your heart? That woman of Samaria claimed and was claimed by Jesus. His thirst evoked a response from her and her thirst got an answer from Jesus. But it didn't end in their noonday interchange. That mutual claim sent her back to her community with questions and a story. Her story and her questions moved hearts in that town of Sychar, and Jesus abided with them two days.

Who's got a hold on you? Whose story is claiming and softening your heart? What questions are rising? Those are God's mission invitations. It's an ancient pattern: when God hears the voices crying in the wilderness, God sends Moses and Aaron and Miriam, and eventually, you and me. When we hear the people cry, they lay a claim on us. That's where we meet Jesus, that's where we share God's love, and that's where we're meant to be.

Who's got a hold on you?

PART TWO

SHALOM, EVERYBODY
The Vision of Peace

City of God

⬥

People often ask me why an Episcopal bishop would sign e-mails with the Hebrew word "Shalom." I tell them that for me it is a continuing verbal symbol and a reminder of what it is I'm supposed to be about, and in fact, what all Christians are supposed to be about.

That word "shalom" is usually translated as "peace," but it's a far richer and deeper understanding of peace than we usually recognize. It's not just a 1970s era hippie holding up two fingers to greet a friend—"Peace, bro." It isn't just telling two arguers to get over their differences. Shalom is a vision of the city of God on earth, a community where people are at peace with each other because each one has enough to eat, adequate shelter, medical care, and meaningful work. Shalom is a city where justice is the rule of the day, where prejudice has vanished, where the diverse gifts with which we have been so abundantly blessed are equally valued.

The biblical image of Jerusalem is a city like that—that's what the "salem" part means. And that word for peace shows up all over the Middle East. Islam comes from the same root, and it means submitting one's will to God's in the search for that just community. The greeting we exchange with each other at the Eucharist is another reminder—"I will be in peace with you, let us be people of peace together."

When Jesus goes back to his hometown and reads that passage from Isaiah in the synagogue and says, "Today this scripture has been fulfilled in your hearing," he's talking about this vision of shalom, the reign of God springing up all around. When he says, "Today, this has happened," he doesn't mean that all the work's been done and finished, that God's reign is fully realized. I don't know about you, but I look around out there and see a fair bit of poverty, lots of prisoners, quite a few people with broken hearts, and lots who have no access to health care. The work is not finished, by a long shot! But we do see signs—interfaith networks and soup kitchens and music that brings balm to wounded souls.

And we don't just see signs in the work that every parish does. Each one of us has the potential to be a partner in God's government, to be a co-creator of a good and whole and peaceful community. Each one of us has been given abundant gifts to do that work. All that's needed is a vision and a heart. The vision is one that Isaiah spells out—a society of peace and justice. The heart is a work in progress for all of us—sometimes a harder heart, sometimes one softened up enough to feel compassion for those who haven't yet experienced that vision of shalom. Along with compassion, our hearts tell us to get off our duffs and use our gifts to do something about those people around us who are in pain, who don't know peace.

When you think about your gifts, consider what you're good at, what gets you up in the morning, where your passion is, what you love about living. For some, it's probably sports—soccer, swimming, golf, tennis, football. What in the world do they have to do with shalom or the reign of God? Whatever we do can be a witness, an example, that leads other people toward sharing our vision of shalom. What's sometimes called old-fashioned sportsmanship is about treating our opponents with respect, and permitting them to have as much dignity as us, both in victory and defeat.

Some people are gifted as teachers, or parents, or mediators. How each one goes about living out that vocation can be part of building the reign of God. In lots of cities, I see people standing on the street selling newspapers, and I usually buy one. Most of the people I meet in that encounter are good ambassadors for what looks to me like the reign of God—they are happy to meet a stranger, and they treat this stranger with respect. The guys I meet do their work with a dignity that denies what most of society would say about them.

In the newspaper recently, there was a series of letters to the editor about a Muslim student who had left high school because of the way she'd been treated. Let's remember that our baptismal covenant does not distinguish between Christians and others—we promise, with God's help, to see and serve Christ in all persons, and respect everyone's dignity, and it doesn't say anything about religion, gender, age, sexuality, nationality, and so on and so forth. The reign of God is not going to be realized until *all* of us can live together in peace. Those letters to the editor were from students at a local high school, inviting the young Muslim woman to join their school, where they believed she would be welcomed. The students who wrote those letters were using a public forum to build a more just society.

That's the kind of work each one of us has agreed to do: to use every resource at hand to build the reign of God—to use the gifts we have, the ones we think we might have, and the ones we haven't discovered yet, to be willing to speak aloud about our vision of peace, whether in the newspaper or the halls of Congress, and to dedicate our lives to making that vision come alive, to give our hearts to it, to believe in it, with every fiber of our being.

Building the reign of God is a great and bold adventure, and it is the *only* route to being fully alive. If we don't set out to change the world, who will?

How Can We Keep from Singing?

A few years ago I visited a nursing home for a special communion service. We read a gospel about eating what is set before you, and I said something to the people gathered about finding the blessing in whatever is offered. (I have to believe that there is great grace in the ability to give thanks for what a nursing home kitchen turns out day after day.) And then we had communion together. Most of the people opened their mouths or put out their hands for the bread, and it was given and received. A couple of folks who didn't respond got a blessing. Afterward, a woman came up and whispered, "That woman over there, the one you just gave communion to, is Jewish!" The woman's son came up to me later and said, "I didn't think I'd ever see my mother take communion!" He seemed both a bit scandalized and rather grateful that she had been included. Somewhere in the depths of her being, underneath the surface confusion, she heard the words about eating what is set before you, and responded. And I am quite certain that *baruch atah adonai eloheinu*—God was praised.

I tell you that story knowing full well that the rubrics were violated, and that some might find it appropriate to bring me up on charges. Yet I think we have to recognize that sometimes the gospel is not about following all the rules. We live in a society that seems consumed with legalisms, penalties, and punishment. Our church is caught up in a struggle over interpretations of scripture that debate whether and how we should be following rules set down long ago.

When Jesus tells the seventy disciples to travel light, and to go and bring good news wherever they are welcome, he is sending them out without their usual supports. They don't get to take along their normal excess baggage, their extra clothes and credit cards, and everything they "just might" need. They are supposed to depend on the hospitality they encounter, on the radical grace present in the world. And if they don't find it, they're supposed to keep on going until they do. And you know, after a long day's walk, maybe without lunch or a coffee break, I think they were probably a lot more willing to look for hospitality in unexpected places. Even the places where the door is already shuttered and the light is off might be a possibility. For when you both need that hospitality, and know and expect that there is grace to be found, you are a lot likelier to keep on looking.

Beginning by saying "peace to this house" is even more likely to bring a positive response. Even a curmudgeon is likely to open up for somebody who comes hat in hand in the middle of a snow storm. The undefended person is not a threat, and grace and hospitality become a likelier response.

Rules can often become fences and defenses that keep some folks safe inside the corral and keep others out. The original genius behind the 613 rules of Torah was about self-definition. By keeping the fullness of that law, the Hebrew people became a nation. Those rules became an occasion of grace that defined their existence and their special relationship to God. Like any other good gift, however, those rules can become an idol, and an excuse for shutting out those human beings we would rather not have in our backyards—or our living rooms. The rules of Christianity or the canons of the Episcopal Church or the laws of this nation are no different—they can be occasions of grace that shape our growth, or they can become dead or even demonic idols.

When Jesus tells the seventy that they have to travel light and receive whatever food is offered, he's taking away all their little comforts and their ability to live by the rules, for the meal of the day just might not be kosher. When they are told to greet the household in peace, it means that whoever lives there is a fit candidate for peace, however that person lives. Peace-bringing and the charge to heal the sickness they find mean that any potential host is capable of wholeness and healing and salvation, and when the disciples can give that greeting with full integrity, then the kingdom of God is close at hand.

What would this world look like if Palestinians were sent off to find hospitality in Israel, and Israelis in Lebanon, and Shiites in Sunni territory? Or Americans in Iraq or Afghanistan? Can you or I go looking for hospitality in the home of an immigrant down the street, whether Mexican or Tongan or Ethiopian? Could we go, two by two, looking for welcome at the home of a paroled murderer or a sex offender?

When Isaiah says "I will give you as a light to the nations," that's the kind of radical hospitality he's talking about. You and I are meant to be light-bearers and shalom-builders, so that God's salvation and wholeness might reach to the ends of the earth. Going looking for hospitality has a lot to do with the hospitality of our own hearts. Can we suspend judgment about where or with whom we might find it?

Ensuring that people keep the rules hedges in the hospitality of our hearts. Yes, we can still be hospitable, but our light only stretches a little way, to the edge of the corral and those who are like us, and it will never reach the ends of the earth. Jesus asks a more radical vulnerability, the kind of vulnerability he himself showed us over and over again, eating with the unclean and the outcasts of his day. He asks of us a welcome that will admit any and every image of God walking this earth.

The harvest is plentiful, those who hunger to give and receive hospitality are abundant, but few are able to set down their loads and go freely in search of the kingdom of God. There are many prisoners waiting to hear "Come out," and many living in darkness, afraid to show themselves. There are countless throngs who hunger and thirst and suffer from wind and sun, who struggle up mountains and through the valley of the shadow of death. Yet God in his wisdom called us in the womb to be servants of peace, to share in the gift of what we find in whatever place we visit, to offer healing, and in that meeting to see and announce the present reign of God.

The harvest is rich and abundant, and we only have to go—tripping lightly, announcing peace. And once we get a taste of it, how can we keep from singing?

I don't think I've ever heard anybody sing rules, or sing about rules. They are vital preparation and discipline, but they are not the goal. We have to be formed by those rules, like a singer who learns scales and breathing exercises, and practices them day after day and year after year, so that when opening night comes his voice can soar. That training sets the artist free to respond to the encounter of the moment, to the rich surprise of an especially responsive audience or an impromptu singing partner in the park.

The harvest, the transforming and liberating gift of the gospel, comes in the ability to see and move beyond our limited perceptions, to see the image of God in this unexpected person before us, however she does or does not keep the rules or fit our fond expectations.

I recall another encounter—a fellow who sat through an entire Christmas Eve service years ago, in the front pew, wearing his ten-gallon hat. The fact that he didn't take his hat off was what was talked about for ages afterward, not the curious and blessed gift of his personality, which we never discovered.

Encountering the stranger as potential friend means that the kingdom of God has come near, and we will continually discover it when we are ready to eat what is offered, when we can find grace in the stew of sea cucumbers or the frijoles or the struggling sinner across the table.

We are meant to be bringers of peace and shalom, a light to the nations. And we are meant to sing a new song of grace and abundance, of healing and transformation.

May God bless our search for hospitality, within our own hearts and in all we meet. Shalom chaverim, shalom my friends, shalom.

Shalom around the World

In John 14:23–29 Jesus tells his friends that he is about to leave them. He's talking about his impending death, even though we usually read this just before the Feast of the Ascension. Jesus isn't going to be around in the same way he's been for the last months and years, and he's leaving final instructions. OK, folks, this is how I want you to carry on. You have God's vision of shalom. Now love each other, and don't be afraid.

It's that last bit that gets in our way most often. We may be able to recover that grand vision of a city of peace for a while, but then something jumps up and bites us—something that disturbs our peace. The Christian life is about learning to let go of those disturbances so that peace comes center stage again. Do we ever manage to do it completely? No, or at least we won't until the second coming, but the peaceful periods can get longer.

I've met with lots of people in many corners of the world who are interested in how to build Christian communities that live out that dream of shalom. My most important learning in the time I've worked on that is that the character of our communities' leaders is what is most central. If the leaders have no peace, the community won't either, and none of them can be effective builders of that dream of God. It's not all the clergy's fault, or all the clergy's responsibility. Baptism, after all, calls us all to be leaders. That bath in the river of life sends us out as builders of the reign of God— we are all ministers of the government of God. Our portfolios are unique, but we all serve the same Lord. You may be minister of education or minister of healing, or minister of child-rearing, engineering, farming, or sanitation. The various places and modes in which we live out our baptismal covenant are all ways toward that dream of God, that city of peace.

Sometimes the ministry to which we are called changes. I spent the first part of my adult life as an oceanographer, studying squids and octopuses in the northeastern Pacific. A time came when I couldn't continue to work as an oceanographer because government research priorities changed. My experience was one of loss, anger, and frustration—I'd spent fifteen years working toward a life-dream, and I was in deep grief over the death of that dream. The subject of ordination came up, but I wasn't ready to hear it. Gradually, through working in my church and for various charities, I came to let go of my old ideas about the path my life would take. Somehow God called me to work where I might be of service, and my grief began to be redeemed.

The dyings in our lives bring new life. That is the centerpiece of our Christian story. It's also the centerpiece of baptism and baptismal ministry. When we walk into that river of life, we die. We come out on the shore raised, renewed, opened to life in a new and different way. In the early Church, those who were being baptized went naked into the font, they were drowned in fairly realistic ways, and they emerged dripping wet to be covered in scented oil and then given a new garment. No wonder it was life-changing! We've gotten a lot more squeamish about public nudity—unless it's advertising or cinema—but in a baptismal experience like that you could not possibly miss the point. Your old life was left behind and you were anointed and robed to emerge as a minister of God.

Going naked into the font says something about your openness and vulnerability to whatever God has in store for you. That's a piece of baptismal leadership that is still central today. Our ability to die to self, to be openly vulnerable to the moving of the Spirit, or to God's latest surprise, is a mark of a growing Christian leader. Where has God surprised you lately?

That's what Jesus is talking about when he says don't be afraid. If you are certain of God's abiding presence, of God's enduring love, then whatever comes, you can be a loving presence in the midst of that experience.

I took a trip to Australia that carried with it some anxieties. I fully expected that sitting in a coach seat on an airplane for fourteen hours would leave me exhausted and terminally grumpy by the time I arrived. What I found was an airplane so empty that I could stretch out and sleep on the seats adjoining mine. I actually enjoyed what turned into a fourteen-hour retreat!

When I arrived I was really quite unsure of what to expect. I knew the basic outline of what my work was to be, but not much more. I anticipated that somebody would pick me up in Sydney and take me to a hotel to park myself until it was time for the first meeting. What I experienced was the incredibly gracious welcome of a couple who lived in Sydney who took me to their home, took me around the sights that afternoon, invited friends in for dinner, and made me feel like I'd encountered the heavenly banquet. It continued on the following day, when we had a spectacular outing through the sights of the Blue Mountains. Again, I really expected to be parked in a hotel for a while, but the bishop I was visiting brought me to his home, introduced me to his wife, and then took us off to another heavenly banquet! Everywhere I turned during that amazing trip I encountered over-the-top and abundantly gracious hospitality. Uncertainties and anxieties evaporated in the glowing presence of Australians. Strangers became friends, and I had the awesome experience of meeting the divine enfleshed at every turn.

The heavenly banquet is all around us, all the time, even if it does turn up in unexpected guises. My peace I leave with you, Jesus says. I am going away and I will come to you. What expectations will we carry with us? Will we expect to find Jesus' love in the folks around us, or in the stranger on the street? Will the grace and power of the resurrection inform our daily living three months from now? Can we let go our fear long enough to be truly surprised by what God is up to in our midst?

May we know the true peace of God's presence that casts out every fear, and may we become Christ's peace, the shalom of God, in each moment of our living.

PART THREE

A BILLION PEOPLE,
A DOLLAR A DAY
Working for Justice and Peace

God Bless the Whole World, No Exceptions

As Christians, we're all about Incarnation—God made flesh and dwelling among us. And, in a very real sense, the feast of the Incarnation continues all year long, and through all the years, more than two thousand of them already.

On this feast of the Incarnation called Epiphany, we hear the stories of the wise men or the three kings coming to visit the baby Jesus. We've usually understood that story to be about Jesus coming for the whole world. In Isa 66:18–23 we hear an earlier vision of God's coming for the whole world. Isaiah tells of the glory of God sent out to all the nations—to Tarshish, Put, and Lud, to Tubal and Javan. We're not completely sure, but those places are probably what we would today call Spain, Libya, North Africa, Greece, and Turkey. In the time of Isaiah those were the ends of the known world. God has in mind to take all these foreigners and make them into servants of a new creation. This is about a new world order, or a global village, or an international community. The kingdom of God, or God's commonwealth, hasn't got room for national chauvinism.

In coming among us in human form, Jesus made God's love evident to all nations and all peoples. All of us have roots in particular ethnic identities, even though many Americans identify more with Heinz 57 than pure Polish or Swedish or Nigerian roots. One of the dreams of the founders of this nation was that people of all national origins might dwell together in peace. But human reality has always targeted one or more groups as "outsiders." A hundred years ago, the Irish immigrants and the Italians and Chinese were the focus of a great deal of that kind of ostracism. Fifty years ago those of Japanese descent faced even more rigid exclusion. People of African and Latin American descent still struggle with second-class treatment in our society. God's presence among us in human flesh is a gift to all the nations. None of us is worthy of the gift, no matter what the color of our skin. But the gift is given nonetheless. None of us had to qualify, none of us had to pass a test. God doesn't require a green card.

I don't know a great deal about my own genealogy. What I know of my mother's family is that supposedly we're descended from Eamon ManOch, or Ned of the Hills. I've been told that he was something like the Irish Robin Hood. On my father's side, the first immigrant to America was a Swedish draft dodger. Both of those ancestors were little people—people who'd known something of the injustices of their societies or governments. The gift for me out of that heritage has been a passion for justice and equal treatment of people of all socio-economic classes. The gifts of your heritage are different, but valuable in many different ways. Each one of us is uniquely gifted for the work of God's commonwealth, and God needs all of us and our gifts.

Have you ever been to a "skinny" potluck? When there wasn't any main dish, or salad, and everybody brought dessert? It usually makes for a good laugh, but it's not very nourishing. The vision of God's reign as a heavenly banquet is a potluck made up of all our contributions. The celestial potluck is supposed to be infinitely rich and abundant. It needs all of our dishes, and it needs dishes we haven't even met yet. Every single person we meet is a contribution to the celestial potluck. Maybe we need to redeem the phrase "What a dish!" as an equal-opportunity invitation to appreciate God's gift in a new person. Just like a new food, try it once, and then again—and maybe even seventy-seven times, till you can find the gift there.

We celebrate the Incarnation all year long, as we look for God's gifts in people of other nationalities and traditions. It's often harder to see the gift in something or someone unfamiliar, so take time to search, and then appreciate what you find. We can look as well for the gifts in our own ancestors—and give thanks. Finally, let's be ready for opportunities to share those gifts. God needs them all!

Doing Is Believing

A couple of years ago, I had the utter delight of waking up and seeing an old friend and colleague on television, talking about the pictures of giant squid he'd taken off Japan. I hadn't seen Tsunemi Kubodera for more than twenty years, but he was still just as passionate about squid as he was when we worked together. He is not a Christian, but he does have a clear sense that his work involves caring for creation.

All of us, called by our baptism, have been given the sense that we're meant to care for some part of creation, whether our family or neighbors or strangers or the animals we bless on the feast of St. Francis. We've heard Jesus' call to be table waiters, servants, and ministers to those around us.

Throughout the church, many are working in some form of healing ministry—pharmacists, childcare workers and foster parents, nurses, and if we can envision healing more broadly, teachers and brokers of knowledge—for that is really what consultants and salespeople are and do. All of them are about helping to make or restore connections—in church language we call that reconciliation. All of them are involved in service to others. Their ministry, particularly the ministry of deacons, is to remind us of the hurts and needs of the world around us. We ordain them in order to urge us and nag us to get involved in healing those hurts and needs, to build and rebuild the communities around us.

Traditionally, we've often understood ministry or service as putting another's needs ahead of our own, but the truth is actually bigger and more comprehensive than that, for ministry has to do with healing the world. Our own healing is bound up in the healing of all. Traditional language would talk about salvation, but the roots of that word are the same as for health and healing and holiness. Good, healthy, and holy ministry involves seeing the healing of one person or a single situation as part of that larger whole. When it's all healed we'll know the reign of God has come in its fullness.

The work we do every day, our daily baptismal ministry, is about healing the world—as Paul says, "Letting light shine out of darkness," or in
Jeremiah's words, doing that for which "we were consecrated before we
were born." Much of the time, our work focuses on the nearby and close at
hand—our families, fellow citizens, co-workers, and parishioners, but we
are part of a much larger whole. After all, when one is in pain, all suffer,
and when one is healed, the whole world breathes a bit easier.

We are beginning to recognize that the cars we drive and fuel we burn
have something to do with storms in the Gulf of Mexico and melting
permafrost in Alaska and rising sea levels that threaten islands in the
South Pacific and the shores of Asia. Recently, the bishop of Bangladesh
attended our House of Bishops meeting, and he asked us to remember
that our actions have major impacts on his low-lying country, which is
increasingly devastated by storms. He said, "Nature is creating weapons
of mass destruction. Do something so we don't have to live with these
curses." We have a small sense of that here in the United States, but even
the devastation that has been felt along the Gulf Coast is puny compared
to the devastation of the Asian tsunami or the tropical storms that lash
the coast of Bangladesh.

But consider the local situation. The winds of Katrina and Rita blew
away the veils that cover the shame we bear in our own land. We are seeing
the systemic evil that isolates people according to race or income or class.
The bishop of West Virginia told me about a number of people who were
evacuated from New Orleans to Charleston, West Virginia. First, they
thought FEMA was taking them to Charleston, South Carolina. And when
they arrived, the local school board said, "Oh, those children just won't fit
in our schools—you'll have to set up something temporary somewhere
else." Racism is not dead in this land. It is not limited to the South or
"those other parts" of the country, or to black-white relations. Bigotry,
prejudice, and racism diminish us all. We will not be healed until Martin
Luther King's dream is realized, until black children and white children
and Hispanic and Filipino and Paiute children can play and learn and
grow up together in peace. There's more than enough room for the ministry of healing in this world of ours.

We are also beginning to recognize that very small actions on our part
can make enormous differences for good in the rest of the world. The Millennium Development Goals are a concrete image of healing in this world.

As we approached the year 2000, a number of leaders prioritized the goals of international aid work—the ministry of nations if you will—in eight broad categories that address the needs of the poorest of the poor.

More than 1 billion people live on less than $1 a day, and most of them are hungry. The first of these goals seeks to eliminate that kind of extreme poverty. The other goals seek to achieve universal primary education, to ensure that equal numbers of girls and boys go to school, to reduce the rate of child mortality (more than 11 million children die every year from preventable disease), to improve maternal health, to provide clean water and basic sanitation, to work to reverse the spread of AIDS, malaria, and tuberculosis, and to develop global partnerships for development. When Jesus said, "When you fed a hungry person, gave water to one who was thirsty, or cared for one who was ill, you did it to me," this is the kind of ministry he was talking about.

The good news is that achieving those big goals is possible—in ten years—with a relatively small investment. Economists calculate that if the advanced nations gave merely 0.7 percent of their national income to international development, we could pretty much eliminate this kind of poverty. In 1998, at a meeting of the bishops of the Anglican Communion, the churches committed themselves to working toward these goals. The Episcopal Church signed on in 2000. Individual dioceses followed suit. The nations of the world haven't caught up yet—only the Scandinavian countries and the Netherlands are giving at that rate. The U.S. gives 0.16 percent of its gross national income—we would need to increase our giving about four-fold to meet the goal. Now 0.7 percent is not a great deal—it's 70 cents out of $100, or $7 out of $1000. Participating in these goals is a witness, an example, and a ministry in itself.

This is an achievable dream. If you want to learn more, I will suggest a book called *What Can One Person Do?*[3] It's short and eminently readable, and it's gospel. For a fuller treatment, consider reading *The End of Poverty* by Jeffrey Sachs.[4]

Our giving can do something about the sixty thousand people who die every day from hunger and lack of basic medical care. Paul says in his wonderful letter, "We have this treasure in clay jars so that it may be clear

3. Sabina Alkire and Philip Newell, *What Can One Person Do?* (New York: Church Publishing, 2005).
4. Jeffrey Sachs, *The End of Poverty* (New York: Penguin Press, 2005).

that this extraordinary power belongs to God and does not come from us." The extraordinary power he's talking about is a result of believing and doing something about that belief. When we know the powerful reality of God's love, we can change the world. The same attitudes that permit or overlook poverty and racism in our towns and cities lead to similar realities in Louisiana and Mississippi, as well as in Asia and Africa. Our neighbors are not just the folks next door, and we are meant to be servants of them all. How we use our abundance is a very real statement about what it is we do believe.

Ministry is another kind of stewardship, for it is about the right use of the gifts we have been given—our intelligence, our hands, our creativity, our passion, and our money—how we use those gifts to care for all of creation, including human beings and giant squid and the earth on which we dwell.

A Cup of Starbucks

❧◈❧

Down in the southern end of the Las Vegas valley they are starting to build roads up into the mountains for what will be very expensive homesites. I was surprised that there weren't any land-use restrictions on that kind of building, given the herds of desert bighorn sheep up there. If you've never seen one of those bighorns, they are quite magnificent. They are about the only kind of sheep that can survive in this part of the world. Domestic sheep need much better grazing, and more abundant water, and lots of human care.

God's relationship to human beings is frequently compared to that of shepherd and sheep. The shepherd goes after the lost, steers them to fresh grazing and water, and protects them from predators. Several years ago my husband Dick and I hiked the Ruby Crest Trail south of Elko, and we saw a great deal of evidence of sheep and shepherds on the last part of the trail. The shepherds up there are no longer Basque, but now often come from South America. Along several miles of trail, we frequently saw carvings the shepherds had made while waiting for their sheep to graze. One fellow's mark turned up repeatedly. We read many times what he had carved in the trees: "Antonio Hidalgo, Peruano, borreguero, con muchos cojones y poco dinero," or loosely translated, 'Antonio Hidalgo, Peruvian, shepherd, with lots of guts but no money!' The lives of shepherds are no different today than they were two or three thousand years ago.

Comparing God to a shepherd is one of those gospel-overturning moves. Shepherds were the lowest of the low, considered ritually unclean, and generally outside the boundaries of polite society. Shepherds have to get dirty to care for their sheep. They may stand watch all night if there are ewes about to lamb, or coyotes hovering near. They are servants of those who need a helper.

Jesus compares himself to a shepherd who's going to separate the sheep from the goats at the end of time. I've always thought that the goats get a bum rap. We kept goats for more than twenty years in Oregon. They are intelligent creatures, wily and independent and creative thinkers, and

51

they don't need anything like the same kind of care that a sheep does. They're hardier, they can survive in a climate like this one, and they can get out of almost any pen human beings can devise if there's a tasty rosebush on the other side. Maybe there's a hint in there about why the goats are less favored in the parable. In Jesus' day, it was common to keep sheep and goats together in the same flock, and sometimes, the shepherd would separate them at the end of the day—goats in this pen, and sheep in that fold over there.

In Jesus' parable, the sheep get the blessing, but not the goats. The fascinating thing is that the sheep, the blessed ones, are simply the ones who take care of the least among us, who feed the hungry, or water the thirsty, or visit the prisoners. The blessed are the ones who act like a blessing—not necessarily the ones who believe correctly, or repeat a statement of salvation, or even keep the fine points of the ritual law. The blessed are the ones who love God and love neighbor as themselves.

I once visited with a Ghanian priest who comes from an incredibly poor place. He's responsible for eighty congregations, and he has no car. He gets up at 3:30 every weekday morning and goes out to stand by the roadside to hitch a ride so that he can go and celebrate communion with his far-flung flock. He says the people are so poor that they must depend on God—they have no one else. He also told me about an encounter between his bishop and some westerners, when the bishop said, "God will judge you—how have you cared for the poor in Africa? How can you live with yourselves as wealthy people, when others are starving?"

How can we live with ourselves when our brothers and sisters are starving? Sometimes the scope of the problem seems so overwhelming that we don't know where to start, so we don't do anything. We get paralyzed. But many parishes know a great deal about feeding the hungry in their own communities. Some know something about caring for the hungry across the globe.

There is increasing cause for hope that some of those hungry ones who need our help will receive it. Our Congress recently passed The Assistance for Orphans and Vulnerable Children Act, which calls for a strategy to address the needs of those children around the globe. In Africa alone, 14 million children have lost one or both parents to AIDS, and by 2010 there could be 25 million. By way of comparison, there are about 14 million children in this country below the age of five. This law commits the U.S. to develop a strategy to provide adequate food and medical care and access to primary education for these at-risk children. People have encouraged Congress to think about the poor across the world, and they have heard us.

The Millennium Development Goals also aim to eliminate extreme poverty in the next ten years. This law about orphans addresses several of those goals, and it has the potential to feed the hungry, clothe the naked, and heal the sick among the least of these. This is an act of sheep, whatever their religious persuasion.

The Goals invite national governments, dioceses, churches, and individuals to give 0.7 percent of their incomes for international development—to make hunger history, to ensure that all children can get a primary education, to see that all the world's people have access to basic health care, clean water, and sanitation. We can eliminate the extreme poverty that afflicts 2 billion people in this world, if we have the will. We can only do it if we work together, if we're willing to act like a flock of sheep rather than a bunch of goats. But even more than sheep, we're asked to be like shepherds for the other sheep around the world and in this land, for the ones that have fallen into a pit, the ones that can't climb out on their own. Jesus, our shepherd king, is willing to get dirty on behalf of the sheep and loves those wanderers beyond all measure of reason. That Peruvian shepherd who carved his poem on so many trees in the Ruby Mountains came to the United States looking for a livelihood. In some measure, he must have found it. While he didn't have much money, he did have the wherewithal to leave a blessing behind him. We shepherds have both the money and the will to do even more—we can change this world into something that looks more like Jesus' sheep live here. Will we feed the hungry and water the thirsty and clothe the naked and welcome the stranger?

Will we respect the dignity of every human being? Will we strive for justice and peace? Will we seek and serve Christ in all persons, and love our neighbor sheep as ourselves?

We can examine how we live and what we believe is so essential, and perhaps re-orient our priorities. The price of a cup of Starbucks' finest once or twice a week would just about meet the goal.

We can continue to feed the hungry and respond to the needs of the homeless and mentally ill right here.

And we can open our hearts and our wallets to our hungry neighbors around the world. While 0.7 percent is only a few hundred dollars a year for most of us, it can truly change the world. And it is a gospel imperative.

Whenever you do it to the least of these, says Jesus, you do it to me.

Sharing the Wealth

There is a bumper sticker, still seen occasionally, that says (in slightly more colorful language), "God is coming, and boy is she ticked!" It's related to the one that says, "Jesus is coming. Look busy."

Lots of religion seems to focus on what the end of things will look like, or how God is going to treat the wrongdoers.

Pat Robertson made the news a while ago when he told the people of Dover, Pennsylvania, that the next time something bad happened to them, God was not going to listen. According to him, judgment has now been pronounced because they had the audacity to recall their school board for banning the teaching of evolution. The Dover folks voted in a new slate, who have promised to restore mainstream science education, and therefore, in Robertson's eyes, they are now beyond redemption.

There is another strand in the tradition, however, a far stronger one.

An old rabbinical story tells about what happens when a person dies. Moses meets the person and asks just one question of judgment, "Have you enjoyed everything God gave you to enjoy?"

That's much closer to what Jesus is talking about in the parable about the talents. What have you done with what you've been given?

A talent was an enormous sum in Jesus' day. It represented a weight of gold, something like seventy-five pounds, or a lifetime's wages for a laborer—hundreds of thousands of dollars. An enormously wealthy master had gone off on a long trip and left his three servants in charge of his fortune. The one who had charge of five talents doubled the investment. The one who was in charge of two talents doubled his allotment, too. But the servant who was given one talent only returned what he was originally given. The master says to the first two servants, "Enter into the joy of your master," but the third is called wicked and lazy for not making more of his talent.

That word "talent" originally meant this vast sum of money, but it has come into our language with a far richer connotation of skills and gifts and abilities. Is this parable about money, or is it about what we call talents today?

The Diocese of El Salvador is poor and rural, with five thousand Anglicans and six clergy gathered in seventeen congregations, and they know something about the devastation of hurricanes. It is a poor country and diocese, not much wealthier than Haiti, the very poorest country in our hemisphere. El Salvador has had partner relationships with several U.S. dioceses, and many, many people from the U.S. have gone there on medical missions and for rebuilding efforts. In late September of 2005, after hurricanes hit the Gulf Coast, the bishop of El Salvador promised that his diocese was going to contribute all of their income from that month to the relief work on the Gulf Coast. All of it, from every congregation in the diocese. Every penny. They know what it is to be the victims of natural disaster, and they are sharing what they have with others who have lost everything. Their knowledge of common suffering prompted a desire to share, and it brings joy to all.

Joy clearly has something to do with using well what we've been given, even risking everything we have. It means living with passion, for as the psalm says, we are like grass that is green in the morning but burnt to a crisp by dusk.

Have you ever known a hoarder, someone who has a clinical disease that makes it nearly impossible to throw anything away? As a hoarder's home fills up with newspapers, magazines, junk mail, old shoes, and plastic food containers "that might be needed some day," life gets smaller and smaller. Depression—vast and deep depression—is usually a part of this disease. That third servant is not unlike a hoarder—he's afraid to get out of his shell of safety and live life with abandon.

He admits that he's afraid of what the master would do to him if he lost the talent. Fear seems to be an issue for lots of us. Fear of change, fear of risk, fear of failing or looking foolish. I'm reminded of what the angel says every time one appears in the Bible: "Fear not." And as Jesus says, "Perfect love casts out fear." Fear gets in the way of abundant living and finding the joy we were created for.

The third servant is told that even if he'd put the talent in the bank he would have found some joy. But to do nothing, not to even try to use it, brings him into that vision of judgment and loss. From those who have nothing, even what they have will be taken away. He had something, but he didn't use it, and now he has nothing.

We've all got enormous gifts. All of us. We may not have identical gifts, but we all have something that can be used to make more—to make more of life, more of God's loving reality, more shalom. Not to use that gift means we opt for the grim side of judgment, the day of the Lord. But it is our choice, our own decision, that brings that kind of judgment.

Everywhere I look I see enormous gifts and talents. There are abundantly gifted people in every community, with mountains of golden ability. But we've also got a long history of not working together very effectively, and I think that challenge is related to the gifts we all have in such abundance. We have enormous potential to change our communities for the better, but it's not going to happen if one person's gifts are competing with another's, saying "I'm right" or "My gift is more important than yours." Remember what happened to Cain and Abel? When Cain brings his offering, and it's not accepted in the same way as Abel's, Cain gets furious. And God says to Cain, "Why this tantrum? Why the sulking? If you do well, won't you be accepted? And if you don't do well, you've got to master it."

The gifts and talents that have been so abundantly showered on us are not ours alone. They are given to us with the understanding that we will act as stewards, guardians, and investors. We're meant to invest them, to risk them, for the good of all. Joy and abundant life come when we're willing to risk all that we have, to lay down our lives.

God has not called us together here to ignore our gifts. At the very least we can collect interest, and even better, we can act like venture capitalists. We're asked to invest what we have in that great dream of God. A tiny fraction of our wealth can radically change the lives of one third of the world's people. But it's not going to happen unless we can act as one body—one Body of Christ, one family of God, one people of all the earth.

We already have an inkling of what is possible when we work together. Think of what more you can do. Could you become a haven for under-occupied children in the hours after school closes? Might you teach more lonely elders about the abundant life to be found in community? Will you become a laboratory of love for families who are consumed by consumerism? All are possible, you can double your gifts and more, if you are willing to risk what you have.

The parable of the talents might be titled, "Use it or lose it!"

God is coming, and we never know when. Judgment comes whether we are ready or not, but judgment is always about our decisions. As the nineteenth-century Swiss philosopher Henri-Frederic Amiel put it, "Life is short and we have not much time to gladden the hearts of those who walk this way with us; so let us be swift to love and let us make haste to be kind."

Let us be swift to love, to use every gift at hand in the service of love, and we, too, shall enter into the joy of God.

Ready for Grace

❖

My husband Dick and I went for a long hike a while ago, on an Oregon Cascades section of the Pacific Crest Trail. We'd only gone about ten minutes down the trail when I thought I saw a deer ahead of us, and I stopped, hoping to see more. When it came out from behind a tree, I could see that it was a man with a fishing pole in his backpack, which I'd mistaken for antlers. When he got close, he sang out, "Buenos dias," and I responded, "Buenos dias, ¿como esta?" He didn't continue in Spanish, but he stopped and it was abundantly clear he wanted to talk. We asked where he was going, and he said, "Canada." Here was one of those PCT hikers who goes from Mexico to Canada in a season stretching over five months! I asked if he'd started at the Mexican border, and he said, "No, Kennedy Meadows, south of the Sierra." He went on to tell us that family issues had interrupted his trip, but they'd been dealt with, and he was still on target to hit Canada by fall. He went on to tell us about the beauty of the trail and the river ahead of us. And then he was gone.

I thought about him as we went down the trail—how long had it been since he'd had words with somebody else? His joy was abundant, but there was a hunger as well. His need for daily bread came in the form of the milk of human kindness and conversation.

Here perhaps was an example of what the Deuteronomist says, "Man does not live by bread alone, but by every word that proceeds from the mouth of God." This guy needed words, and he seemed to be satisfied with whatever he could get from other human beings.

We often call Jesus the Word made flesh. Jesus says he is the living bread come down from heaven. Jesus is the Word-bread—he is bread for living, and as God, he comes in whatever form is most needed. When you and I attempt to live into that baptismal promise about proclaiming good news in word and deed, that is what we are meant to emulate. We are supposed to be bearers of daily word-bread for the hunger of our neighbors.

That's why we're at the Eucharist week after week, and it is what we are sent out to accomplish in the days between.

Word-bread to feed our neighbor's hunger. Like so much of our journey, it's utterly simple, and astoundingly challenging.

Deuteronomy challenges us to live by every word that comes from God. Jesus sums it up as loving God and loving our neighbors as ourselves. Paul gives particulars, like dealing with our anger, and choosing our words with love and graciousness, and giving up bitterness and wrath and wrangling and slander, and choosing kindness and forgiveness.

Whichever way we look at it, it is about sharing the bread we have with those who have none. Those who believe, who give their hearts to this word-bread kind of good news, will live in God's presence and know it.

What kinds of hunger do you know or see? What hungers around you need that word-bread?

I once served as chaplain to high schoolers at Nevada's diocesan camp. The week began, as it usually does, with forty-five two-legged bags of hormones negotiating turf and relationships. Pants that couldn't ride any lower without falling off, and tops that showed more than they covered. A boy with blue hair fading into his more-usual brown, and a girl with blond hair on top and bright pink in the back. Makeup more suitable for—hmm, somewhere else—and T-shirts that proclaimed all sorts of questionable allegiances. And all of it is about finding a place in this world. Finding a place to be valued, to belong, to be loved and respected. The outrageous outsides are about uncertain insides, and they most definitely need feeding. In chapel we talked about heaven—what it is, where we find it, how we might experience it and contribute to it. Through the week, as kids went hiking and to the beach, stayed up late to play pranks, and ate awesome meals together at big tables, some of that crusty façade began to brush off. They began to feed each other's hungers in profoundly healing ways—at least in morsels and snacks and appetizers.

Because that's really all any of us can do—offer a taste, and expect that God will do the filling. Taste and see that the Lord is good—and here, let me show you where you can find more.

What kinds of hunger do you see around you?

One-third of the world's people go to bed hungry every night, girls are far less likely than boys to receive a primary education, expectant mothers don't receive adequate prenatal care, and in many countries there's no clean water or adequate sanitation. There are preventable diseases like AIDS, malaria, and tuberculosis that need to be treated. There are hungers all around us, and we can make the world a much different place by 2015 if we set ourselves to the task. We can bring the world closer to the promised land scripture speaks about, a good land where people may eat bread without scarcity, where people will lack nothing, where they can eat their fill and bless God.

The deepest hunger in our world is that all people might have the hope of living in such a land of peace and plenty. The strife in the Middle East, the threat of terrorist attacks, the ongoing wars in Iraq and Afghanistan, the plight of prisoners at Guantánamo Bay—all cry out for the word-bread of peace and shalom. If you and I are fed here with that bread that announces peace, how will we respond? Many communities have a proud history of building shalom among people who come from across the globe to live and study here. Reaching beyond the safe bounds of people we know, and people who are like us, can be one way to respond to that gnawing hunger. If we can see that God in Jesus is drawing the whole world to himself, why do we have so much trouble following suit?

When we eat of this bread, it truly can relieve those fears that keep us turned inward. It truly can engender courage to reach beyond our comfort zones to feed others. But only if we believe, in the root sense of what that word "believe" means—to give our hearts to that truth. We can help to feed the world's hunger only if we invest our hearts, and minds, and souls, and strength in sharing that word-bread with the world.

The bread is baked, and dinner is almost ready. Are we ready for grace?

PART FOUR

FUNNY PURPLE SHIRTS
The Church in the
New Millennium

Walking on Water

Have you ever had one of those dreams where somebody's after you, and you try to scream for help, but you just can't get a sound out? The disciples did, out on the lake, trying and trying to row their boat across. They weren't getting anywhere, a storm was blowing up, and suddenly there was a ghost in the neighborhood. *Help!!!*

And then Jesus climbed into the boat.

I remember nights at sea in a storm. On one cruise, we were out on Oregon State's 150-foot research vessel, trying to take samples from the bottom of the Pacific Ocean. When the waves got too high to put the gear overboard, we put all the equipment away and went inside to wait out the storm. Some people retired to their bunks, sicker than dogs. A couple of them had never been to sea before, or had never seen waves higher than the ship. There was reason to be frightened, if you wanted to dwell on it. Some of the rest of us wanted to ignore the weather. We were rather more blasé—we went down to the mess and played bridge all night.

How do we react in the middle of the night? When we are sick unto death, or scared out of our wits? Those disciples certainly had one answer: stick together, for the community is likely better able to cope than any one person.

That little community in the boat is a pretty good image for the church. John Wesley might have called it a holy club, if not a sailing crew or a cell group. We do not go out into the storm alone. All of us, lay and ordained, are in the same boat. The church as a whole is beginning to remember that we are a body—a body with only one head—and that the body depends on the gifts of all its members. All the members of the body are ministers, not just the ordained. The Methodist Church, even in its Anglican and Methodist Episcopal roots, has probably done a better job at leaving behind some of the trappings of hierarchy, but the job isn't done until every baptized person can claim the title "minister of Christ."

Each time we renew our baptismal covenant, we publicly affirm our desire and will to live together as a community, and to work toward building God's reign in this life. The task of the ordained is to continually hold up that dream of God's, in partnership with all the baptized, holy people of God. The ordained are both set apart from the laity, and still part of it. At times they may serve as the coxswain of some crew, but they also help to row the boat. The expectations laid on them should not be fundamentally different from what we expect of every person on the path to holy living. What is distinctive relates to the gifts they have been given: gifts of leadership, the ability to gather people around God's table, and the courage to speak truth in language that is, as the English reformers insisted, "understanded of the people."

What does it mean to be a leader of God's people? Isaiah says that the leader is fundamentally a servant. Jesus insisted on servanthood as well, washing the feet of his disciples, feeding them, riding a donkey rather than a horse, coming to birth in a stable, and teaching through invitation rather than proofs. God became a servant in Jesus. That is the model of Christian leadership. The role of servant leader may look impossible at first glance—how in the world are we going to transform the world if we can't stand in the street and raise our voices? How are we going to walk the stormy sea with Jesus? How, in this fragile mortal flesh, will we walk to Calvary?

The leader of God's people lives in an open boat, a place where the Spirit can blow through at will, where the table companions are those who have been thrown together in this particular lifeboat. The leader of God's people lives in that open boat, filled with the same hope and faith that were the disciples' when they recognized Jesus in their midst.

It doesn't take much convincing to get someone to come aboard a lifeboat in a storm, but leaders of the church have—in some ways—a more difficult task. They're charged with gathering their communities to feast at God's table. Our tradition insists that all people are invited by Christ to share in the banquet, without regard to any of the distinctions we human beings use to pigeonhole one another. Those disciples didn't throw anybody overboard when the wind came up—they knew they needed all the rowers they could find. And all of us on this earth are in the same lifeboat. All of us have the same task, to value the gifts of every member of the human race, and to engage each one in the service of God's great dream.

We are challenged, however, to go out into the streets and compel the guests to come in. I recognize that compulsion is not a popular word these days. But what if we think about compelling the guests to come in as a challenge to change the party so much, make it so attractive and compelling, that those who are hungry come flocking to our wide-open doors? Making a compelling party is the task of the whole Christian community, not just of the ordained. It's a task that should reach beyond denomination and personal friendship.

I was in Mexico a couple of years ago, working on my Spanish. I met with some Anglicans, who told me stories about the competition they experienced from their Roman Catholic brothers, who, in a couple of communities, routinely stand out on the street before Sunday services, ringing a hand bell to dissuade the faithful from entering any other church. Their fondness for telling these stories gives some clue that the Anglicans could do a lot more reaching out, too.

What about the legendary behavior of the faithful at coffee hour? Jesus himself could walk into many churches and be ignored, and, indeed, is forgotten and missed when we fail to engage the stranger. Inviting people to the feast is not about making my table more attractive than yours, and it's not about eating only with your friends. It's about transforming this world so that the party goes on all the time, so that the banquet feeds everyone. It's about *tikkun olam* —"the repair of the world"—and all creation living in shalom.

That is the truth that leaders are asked to proclaim—the truth of God's great dream, the truth of God becoming servant in Jesus, the truth of love that knows no bounds.

Like the servant of whom Isaiah speaks, our leaders will be expected to lift their voices in the cause of that truth, but without causing a riot in the street. Somehow, I don't think that's too different from walking on water. . . .

What sort of truth would you speak to those disciples in the boat? "Row harder"? Or "Dawn is just around the corner"? Or "Eek, a ghost!"? Or would you remind them, "We are not alone"? All of us, lay and ordained, face nights like that one in the boat, as do the communities and nations around us. Our common task is to continue to proclaim that we are not alone, that we are usually afraid of the wrong things, and that God is continually doing a new thing, if we would only sit up and notice.

Christian leaders have to learn to deal with fear. The ability to proclaim truth, even when you're scared to death, is probably the most critical gift of Christian leadership. It is a gift given to many, not just ordained leaders. The saints we remember are the ones who have lived courageously holy lives—Mother Teresa, Martin Luther King Jr., John Wesley, Dorothy Day, Desmond Tutu. "Take heart," says Jesus, "it is I, do not be afraid." Take heart, whether the challenge is a dark and stormy night, or the suicide of a child in the community, or the need to wrestle again with ordaining gay and lesbian Christians. Take heart when the next unfamiliar situation looms. Take heart when faced with change, for that is the only route to growth in more abundant life.

The only proper place for fear, says the author of the letter to the Hebrews, is this: "It is a fearful thing to fall into the hands of the living God." An encounter with the awesome otherness of God, and the challenges that meeting lays upon us, are truly awesome things. D. H. Lawrence was right when he said, "It is a fearsome thing to fall into the hands of the living God, but an even more fearsome thing to fall out of them,"—though I don't believe we can fall out of God's hands.

Ministers of word and sacraments are charged with equipping the saints to live out their baptismal ministry. The best way to do that is to live a fearlessly holy life, with whatever particular gifts God has given, helping and challenging and encouraging—that word means "take heart"—communities to make a compelling feast, and to speak the truth of God's overwhelming love in all things. Any leader who can do that, in quiet or bold ways, will hear, "Well done, good and faithful servant." Any leader who can encourage a community to live that way will hear, "Sit at my right hand, in the place prepared from the beginning of the world." Good and faithful servants will more often find themselves in that boat, in the middle of the night, than sitting on the beach on a sunny afternoon. Those who would sit in the honored places will face a baptism like that of Jesus, a baptism that takes fear and anxiety and the chaos of feeling unloved and abandoned, and transforms it into sure and certain confidence that God is there in the midst of it all. With that conviction, we can run and not be weary, and walk without fear—even when we're asked to walk on water!

Finding God
in the Differences

◁◈▷

Sometimes when I travel, I have to go dressed up in my funny-colored shirt and collar. Once in a while, something pretty amazing happens. A few years ago, I was flying out of Las Vegas, and I walked into the airport to check in at the ticket counter. There were only a couple of people standing in the line, but the labyrinth lanes were set up between me and the counter. I dodged under a couple of the tapes so I wouldn't have to go all the way around. I got to the end of the line, and there in the distance came a Buddhist monk in his saffron robe. He caught my eye, grinned at me, and made a little bow. When he got closer, I held up the tape so he could go under. We couldn't talk to each other, but we had a sense—I know I did —that we were in the same business and part of the same human community.

A few days ago, I left my hotel to go to a meeting in New York. I told the doorman I needed a cab, and he flagged one down while I was getting my suitcase down off the curb. He opened the door and said something to the cabbie, and helped me get my suitcase into the trunk. As I started to climb into the back, I looked at the driver and discovered that this cabby was a woman, a Muslim woman in a headscarf. We smiled at each other and said good morning, and I told her where I needed to go. When we got there, I paid her, and she gave me back the change. I tried to give her a tip, but she said, "No, keep it—I know you are someone who thinks about God. Thank you." The only thing that I could think of to say was, "Allah u akbar," which means God is great or good. I felt much blessed.

On the way home from that meeting, my plane stopped in Chicago, and everyone except me and another person at the other end of the cabin got off. We had a few minutes, and then the hordes started to descend. One woman came to my row and indicated that she had the window seat, so I got up and let her in. As I started to sit back down, her partner arrived and said she was sitting in the middle. I think these two women were a couple—sixtyish, one black, one white, and they held hands for a good part of the flight. The sad thing to me is that we didn't talk to each other; they seemed to want to avoid me.

Now, I think I met God in each of these encounters. We human beings are created in God's image—and I think I saw a reflection. The first two meetings were more mutual—there was a sense that we recognized that in each other. But the two women on the plane seemed to see me as threatening.

There are all kinds of ways we meet God. There are all kinds of ways we understand God (or don't understand God, which is probably a lot closer to the truth).

Moses meets God in the burning bush—something extraordinary gets Moses' attention, and he discovers that it's God calling. God tells him to take off his shoes, because he's standing on holy ground. I have a friend who always takes off her shoes for communion, because it's holy ground. Those first two encounters—with the monk and the taxi driver—were like standing on holy ground, too. All of us recognized that this surprise meeting was a reminder that we reflect God to one another and the community, and that we are part of the same human community, no matter how we understand God.

When Nicodemus comes to see Jesus, it's a lot more muddled. He comes at night, which is probably the writer's way of saying that he was in the dark or he didn't get it. Nicodemus is interested in Jesus and what he's teaching, but he can't get past his usual way of seeing things. "How can I be born again?" he asks. "I'm already a grown-up." But as Jesus always seems to be doing, he tells Nicodemus that if he wants to meet God, he's going to have to let go of those old understandings and see things in a new way. "The wind/spirit blows where it wants to," he answers Nicodemus, "and you can hear it, but you'll never know where it came from or where it's going." God is always doing more surprising things than we can imagine, right in our midst, if we're willing and ready to notice.

That's probably the biggest hint we get about the Trinity—God is always more, and more mysterious and surprising, than we can imagine. The early theologians talked about the three in one as a circle dance—God who creates, and the human face of God, and the way God continues to come into our lives, unbidden and unexpected. We experience God in different ways because God is most fundamentally relational.

About fifteen years ago theologian and Roman Catholic nun Sandra M. Schneiders wrote a famous paper entitled, "God Is More Than Two Men and a Bird." We may use the language of Father, Son, and Holy Spirit. Old man, young man, the dove or the bird. But it's just language—it hints at, or points toward, the ways in which we experience God, but it can never fully describe God.

Moses was afraid to look at God because he had an intuitive understanding that he couldn't possibly take in the fullness of who and what God is.

What Nicodemus learns is that if he thinks he knows who God is and what God is all about, then he's several cards short of a full deck. He cannot predict what the fullness of God is like from just the few cards he has. He has to be willing to let go of his fixed and unchanging ideas. He has to be willing to engage the Spirit and be surprised. We discover God in wrestling with what the Spirit brings—the very wind blows us off our secure footing.

God is revealed in relationships. God's own self is about community. God is the one who created us with the freedom to choose to enter community. God is not about control. We don't have to be in community, but relationships are the only place we're going to learn what wholeness, holiness, or salvation is really about. God draws us into community, invites us, even lures us, but God does not pull strings to get us into relationship, and God does not compel us or shame us into it.

I think those two women on the airplane, seeing me in my clerical garb, were afraid of me or of how I might judge them. Another meeting I attended recently was a lot like that. I went to a gathering that had been called by two bishops. They had invited every American bishop, but other than me and one other, the ones who came were the ones who are worried about the increasing inclusiveness in the Episcopal Church. Some of them were absolutely furious that New Hampshire had elected Gene Robinson, an openly gay priest, to be their next bishop. The meeting was originally called because of their fears that the church would approve rites for blessing same-sex unions. What I saw in that room looked an awful lot like Nicodemus, afraid of where the Spirit might be blowing next, and unable to predict or control it.

Do we have a clear consensus as a church? No, but as Anglicans, and Episcopalians, we have always held up the idea that there has to be room for those who disagree. We have always prided ourselves on our broad-mindedness and our ability to include those of varying opinions. For it is in learning to live in that difference and disagreement that we begin to find God. There is no merit or growth or wholeness in loving people who agree with us. When we can look at the person next to us who has a radically different opinion, and see the image of God, then we begin to discover that God is more than we can imagine.

What if the next time we meet somebody out there who doesn't look like us or think like us our first reaction were, "Oh, that must be the image of God!" I think that is the Spirit blowing where it will. What am I going to learn about this mysterious God in our church and in the community at large?

Traveling Light

⋘◇⋙

There are two philosophies of camping—take everything but the kitchen sink (and sometimes even an inflatable tub for washing dishes), or take less than you know you're going to need. I tend to err in the former direction; my husband prefers the latter. The last time we went backpacking, there were five in the party. I spent a couple of weeks planning the meals, making sure that there was a gracious plenty. I picked up my pack the first day, and I'm sure it weighed sixty pounds. By the next morning, I'd given up a good part of the food bags to the larger and stronger members of the party. I have a real horror of running out of food. I'm not entirely sure where it comes from, but it's one of those protections that I find it very hard to let go of.

On the other hand, Dick tells a story about a climbing trip he took twenty or thirty years ago. He likes to make one-pot dinners—you know, make some soup, eat some of it out of the pot, then throw in some protein and some kind of carbohydrate and make a stew with what's left. It came to the last day of the trip, and the larder was empty—he had a tin of kippered herring and a package of instant coconut cream pudding. As he tells the story, he said, "Protein and carbohydrates—that'll go together." But even he couldn't eat it. Something tasty was at that point more important than just something to eat.

Jesus tells the disciples to "travel light." This is one of those wonderful stories that work at all sorts of levels—physical, emotional, spiritual, even social. Many of us carry around sixty-pound packs because that's where we find our security. Oh, I might need that, so I'd better hang on to it.

The consumer culture we live in is based on that kind of anxiety: the need to have the latest item, or the newest style, or the biggest gas guzzler. That's where we put our trust—and it is in large part what makes our economy go around. It's a pretty insidious message—young children can tell you what brand of peanut butter or cookies they want, and before much longer, they know what kind of sneakers are "in." Even some governments prey on this inner hunger to have more—look at the incredible amounts of money spent on lotteries and other state-sponsored gambling. The plea to lighten up cuts to the very heart of where many of us find our security and our deepest hopes. Do we believe what it says on the dollar bill? Or do we trust in that green piece of paper or our bank accounts or pieces of plastic?

There are lots of opportunities to lighten up. If you're interested in unloading some surplus possessions, and you've got enough of them, maybe you can put on a big garage sale. In a former parish, they call that the ministry of transition, but transformation might be a better word.

Clean out the attic, garage, and the clutter, and see how much lighter you feel, how much more centered your life becomes. We surround ourselves with other kinds of excessive protection. Some of us carry extra pounds of flesh because eating is a way of protecting ourselves from the cares of the world. Others use different substances—alcohol, nicotine, drugs—or behaviors that betray our lack of trust. Lots of us work too hard, because we believe that's where our ultimate worth lies.

Some of us carry around loads of excess baggage in the form of emotional defenses that separate us from other human beings, or old ways of thinking that only serve to tell us our limits, that keep us living in the past rather than in a radically open future. Some of us put our trust in our pre-judgments of those around us, especially those who differ from us: "Oh, it's not worth building a relationship with that kind of person. She doesn't have anything to offer me," or "He's not worth it."

In the year 2000, the theme of Episcopal Church's General Convention was the year of jubilee—setting slaves free, pardoning debts, and providing for a time of rest and fallowness. In some way or other, those themes are all involved in lightening up. We are slaves to those big backpacks; we are in many ways bound to those who owe us something. Work and busyness are heavy burdens for many of us.

What struck me most at the convention was the incredible diversity of this church. The banners that hung at the entrance to the convention center and behind the altar contained a series of faces, and the message "Behold the Face of God." The banner at the entrance to our worship space was a fifty-foot portrait of Jesus—made up of hundreds if not thousands of small pictures of people. The tables at which we sat for Eucharist each morning held about eight people—at mine were the bishop of Central Ecuador, a

Cuban who used to be bishop of Venezuela and is now a bishop in Atlanta, an Episcopal Church Women delegate from Honduras, and folks from New Jersey, Kentucky, Maryland, and Oregon. With some translation, we could all more or less understand each other, and we worked at hearing what God was saying to the church. Each of us was changed in the encounter.

During the committee hearings and the work of the house of deputies we heard accents from all over—Southern, down-east and Harvard Yard, New York, the French of Haiti, Caribbean English, folks whose roots are in Scotland and England, several sorts of Spanish-speakers, Navajo, Hawaiians, Native Alaskans, an Italian, and Africans from several different countries. That's the Episcopal Church. No initial judgment based on sound is going to be adequate—if you're going to hear the voice of God, you simply have to let go of your initial assumptions about who is speaking and listen to the rich diversity.

Traveling light means going with open hands and open hearts, ready to embrace what the moment offers. It means traveling undefended, without rigid expectations or weapons or high walls of self-defense. Finding a welcome has something to do with being vulnerable, being open to the hospitality that another offers. If we're not ready to receive, if our hands aren't open, then who's going to be able to get in?

Fred Phelps and his gang from Kansas demonstrated one day during the convention. His is the group that went to the funeral of murdered Wyoming college student Matthew Shepard and celebrated, with placards saying Matthew was roasting in hell because he was gay. The saddest part is that whole families stood on the street shouting obscenities—even small children are coached in foul language. I found myself wondering what enormous fear must lie behind such behavior. What's going to break down those walls? Probably the willingness to sit and hear the fearful story. Some of us are sent to preach peace to Fred Phelps and his clan. The only question is, how long do we stay before we dust off our feet and move on?

Traveling light means going with hearts open enough to hear the pain behind Fred Phelp's behavior. Traveling light means having a compassionate heart that can see God in each and every one of our neighbors. That kind of heart only beats freely when we've dumped the excess baggage, when we've begun to feel our own vulnerability. What suitcase, backpack, or old tape can we set down this week? What are we going to take to the garage sale or the garbage dump—or the altar?

Lab Report

The water in our baptismal fonts is a symbol of our unity, our oneness. The hard reality, however, is that we are divided. All of us have parts of our lives where we experience alienation, whether it is siblings who won't talk to us, co-workers who wage a silent and angry battle, or fellow parishioners who believe that an armed truce is the best we can do. If we look beyond our borders, the division is even more evident. We are at war in Iraq, we are still fighting for peace in Afghanistan, and the world's conflicts continue unabated. Even the Anglican Communion is in the midst of some pretty profound disunity, with primates lobbing fiats of disfellowship, edicts of impaired communion, and, when all else fails, intercontinental ballistic bishops. This is not the friendly rivalry of a game of pick-up basketball. It is the grievous division of Joseph and his brothers.

I've been reading the daily meditations of Episcopal priest and writer Tom Ehrich for years, most recently as e-mail. His insight has been that the great sin of the church is the desire to be right. The desire to be right is probably the underlying cause of most of the divisions we experience, in church and out. The siblings who won't communicate are often nursing old wounds over who was right and who was wrong. As a nation we're sorting out who was right and wrong about Saddam's weapons of mass destruction. The rhetoric in the Episcopal Church has often been about who's right and who's not.

In the Diocese of Nevada, the deep divisions are conflicts between the old power of the northern end of the state and the upstarts in the south—isn't it better to have deep and historical roots than the cancerous growth of Las Vegas? Aren't the congregations who employ seminary-trained clergy somehow better and more right than those who have come to employ the gifts of many lay members in providing local spiritual leadership? (Believe me, the opposite opinion is held in many places.) Not long ago, I heard a vestry member say, "Well, I came from that parish over there, and, well, you know, this congregation is just . . . healthier." For *healthier*, you could substitute *better, more correct, perfect*, or *right*. There is an ancient instinct within us that says the way we live, or what we believe, is right, and therefore those folks over there must be wrong. That instinct is probably an ancient survival mechanism, one that predates higher consciousness. It's part of what some of the psychologists call our "snake brain," that part of us that kicks in before we start to think.

That snake brain is highly useful when it comes to saving our skins, because it does kick in before thought. But it's usually destructive when it comes to human relationships, because it only exacerbates turf wars. It's the part of me that fires off when my airspace is violated by cigarette smoke—or when the passenger in the next seat on the airplane begins to overflow into mine. It's the part of the brain that drives road rage. The more the conflict begins to resemble defending our bodies and our lives, the more difficult it becomes to respond out of some higher consciousness. It's not impossible, but it takes a great deal of practice.

And practice is what we are about. What sort of religion do you practice? We won't get it perfectly right until the Second Coming, but we also always have another opportunity. This community called the Church is a laboratory for lovers. If we can learn to love each other here, we can transform the world. If we can begin to believe that we are loved for who we are, beyond all understanding and measure, maybe we can be a little less defensive, a little less snakelike, when we're confronted with a threat.

At its best, Anglicanism has always held up comprehensiveness as one of its highest values. We don't all have to agree. There can be more than one right answer. This turf is God's, not ours, and it's broader and more expansive—even greener—than we are capable of imagining. We have said, from our Celtic Christian beginnings, and explicitly from at least the time of Elizabeth I, that the middle way, the middle road, is the most important, because there is something vital to be gained and learned from the people on both shoulders. Gamaliel, the perennial pragmatist in the book of Acts, says, "Well, what you're about may *not* be right, but we'll just have to wait and see what comes of it. If it is of God, then there won't be any stopping it."

God in Christ is our peace. In Jesus we are made into a body, one body. But we are not made into uniform creatures, all with the same characteristics, gifts, and ways of being. Can you imagine a football team made up of only quarterbacks—or place-kickers? They'd lose every game. What happens when a farmer grows the same crop in the same field year after year? It quickly exhausts the fertility of the soil or it succumbs to insects and diseases—or both. George Orwell, in his novel *1984*, began to imagine for us what a monochromatic human culture would look like. Such a society is totalitarian, prone to violence, and finds it very difficult to be creative or produce new life.

It may be more comfortable to live where everyone agrees with us, but it also quickly becomes boring, stagnant, and dead. Living with people who disagree with us may be challenging, but it is the only route to creativity. The fruit of those challenging relationships will be far more than any one of us could accomplish in isolation. When Jesus says that being angry with our brothers and sisters makes us liable to judgment, that's what he means—we lose our ability to really live, and to be creative builders of the reign of God. When we insult and reject the people we disagree with, we just make it worse—we exile ourselves from that creative community of godliness. We put ourselves in hell.

Reconciliation takes a different kind of dying. If we want to learn to live with the folks who make us most angry, we have to learn to value the differences between us, and maybe even their hate toward us. Joseph said to the brothers who tried to kill him, "You meant it for harm, but God turned it to good." Joseph let go of his fear, maybe because he had some empathy for what his brothers were now experiencing.

Louie Crew, one of the great Anglican activists of recent years, put up a story on the Web that told of his meeting with a school of chaplains years ago. One of the participants, a man named Ernest Gordon, had been a prisoner of war on the River Kwai. Louie asked the chaplain how he had survived that brutal prison camp, and Gordon replied,

> "I practiced the discipline of remaking the face of each torturer into the face his mother had seen cuddling him in her arms," he said. "It is very difficult to be swallowed in bitterness when you can do that, and it is the bitterness that would have killed me, even had I lived." (*Through the Valley of the Kwai*)

An invitation: Close your eyes for a minute. Think of somebody whose opinions or actions or very self you reject, find repulsive, or someone with whom you are really angry. Maybe it's a member of your family. Or someone in your congregation. Or the person next to you. It's more difficult to engage with a person who is outside your usual sphere of living—like a politician or world leader—but it's still possible. Hold that person in your mind's eye. Look well. This is a child of God. This is God's beloved, even if it's not easy to see that just yet. If you can't let go of your anger with this person right now, your prayer could be for understanding. "O God, let me see your image in this person I find so difficult. May this person see your image in me as well."

Another invitation: Make this person the focus of your prayers for a week. And when you come again to the Lord's table, maybe, just maybe, there will be some new life in that relationship.

Sibling Rivalry

❧◈❧

James of Jerusalem was in the news recently—did you catch the reports? An ossuary was found in Israel that bears the inscription, "James, son of Joseph, brother of Jesus." It was thought to have dated from roughly 63 C.E., the same year we believe that James died, apparently looted from a grave in Jerusalem. Though scholars and scientists later recognized the ossuary as a very sophisticated hoax, for a while it caused a great stir.

People were excited about the find because it seemed, for a while, to be the earliest written or physical reference to Jesus. James's ossuary wouldn't normally have included his brother's name—most of the other examples of ossuaries tell just the name of the person whose bones they contain, and perhaps the person's father. Even in death, James' fame comes second to his brother's.

James was one of Jesus' several brothers. He apparently wasn't all that sure about his brother until after the resurrection, when Jesus appeared to him. Jesus' family relationships weren't always sweetness and light. You remember the story that tells about his family coming to bring Jesus home, because they thought he was a bit off his rocker. Jesus asks the crowd, "Who is my mother and my brother?" And the answer is, "Those who do the will of God." James came back into the family after Jesus died.

We know a little bit more about James than the names of his siblings—he was the first bishop, in Jerusalem in the late 50s or early 60s. As Sam Portaro puts it, it was "hardly a cushy job, for the episcopate had not yet achieved the splendor it would eventually attain."[5] (I think he must be talking about the Middle Ages—it doesn't seem that splendid now!)

James was a wonderful model of what it means to be a servant leader. I like to tell people that bishops walk at the end of the parade because they have the same job as anybody who walks at the end of a parade— you know, those folks who carry a shovel and bucket. It's the clean-up

---

5. Sam Portaro, *Brightest and Best* (Cambridge, Mass.: Cowley Publications, 1998).

detail. But it's a ministry that's not unique to bishops—it's part of our baptismal covenant. Reconciliation work is cleaning up the messes that exist in this world.

James did it by lowering the bar for Gentile followers of Jesus. No longer would they be expected to live as observant Jews—they would not have to obey all the details of the dietary laws, and the men among them would not have to be circumcised.

James was a reconciler and a visionary. He realized that these problematic Gentiles were also followers of Jesus, and he proposed a compromise to keep the increasingly diverse community of Christians together, even though the parts of it might live under different rules. The Cursillo movement (a renewal movement that, as its name says, is a "short course in Christianity") has become a similar community—the Roman Catholics have one set of rules, the Episcopalians another, the Lutherans yet a third, and so on. Yet they all recognize a common heritage. I don't know who the James was who had a vision that reached beyond the Spanish men for whom the short course was created, but he or she or they certainly existed.

On James' feast day, we pray that we might follow James' example, that we might give ourselves continually to prayer and to the reconciliation of all who are at variance and enmity. That's a not a bad summary of our baptismal covenant—pray and reconcile. Prayer to facilitate our own reunion with God, so that we can go out into the world and live that reconciliation.

For James, that reconciliation didn't happen until after Jesus' death. James must have grown up in his brother's shadow, or at least felt the intense discomfort of having a sibling who didn't fit the social norms. How would you feel if your brother made a habit of eating at soup kitchens instead of coming home for Sunday dinner with the family? We don't know whether James simply played second fiddle to his brother, or if the family would have preferred to disown him. But sometime after the resurrection, James "got" it. He had an encounter with the risen Christ, and he became one of the early leaders of the Christian community in Jerusalem. Reconciliation began for him at the most intimate level of family, and it continued to move out into the larger community. His action in welcoming Gentile Christians under different norms continued a revolution of inclusion that Jesus urged and expanded, a revolution that is not over yet.

In all our lives, in many different ways, we've experienced some kind of reconciliation, some healing or inclusion or restoration. That experience was at least partly the gift of other people in our communities, teaching and supporting us, showing us love in concrete ways, and holding us up in prayer.

Reconciliation comes as the fruit of prayer, vision, and hard work.

What needs reconciliation in your world? Who or what is at variance or enmity? Who is being excluded? Is it a broken relationship with a family member, co-worker, or neighbor? Is it our national state of armed readiness, or our belligerence toward other nations? Is it a division in your church community? Is it the reality of people sleeping on the streets in your city? Is it an attitude of otherness toward people who aren't just like us?

I sat in the airport recently, waiting hours longer than I expected, for an airplane that was late in arriving. A fellow across the waiting area had his cell phone plugged into his ear and carried on multiple conversations at high volume for hours. I heard far more than I wanted to, but at some point my annoyance gave way to amusement. He certainly didn't expect to, but he was doing his part to unite all the people waiting at that gate.

Let's invite those broken parts of our lives into the forefront of our concern, let's make them the focus of our prayer, and then perhaps we'll be ready to do some hard work to bring them together. Bring those divided things to mind, and hold them in your consciousness with care.

What would those divisions look like if they were reconciled? What's your vision of healing? You may not be able to see that in its fullness— maybe it's pretty fuzzy. I don't think James had any understanding of how the early inclusion of Gentile Christians would change the Jesus movement, he just knew that somehow they must be included. All we really need is a drive toward wholeness, a vision that includes reunion, even if we don't know what the details are going to look like. The details are God's problem, not ours.

The hard work to bring about reconciliation comes in lots of forms, and it usually involves some kind of change in us. Maybe, like James, we have to build a compromise, or continue to advocate for the vision we hold, as he did. He did it for decades, and the time came when the authorities in Jerusalem invited him to repudiate that vision from the wall of the Temple. He refused, they pushed him off, and stoned his dead or dying body.

Perhaps our work of reconciliation means we'll have to tell a hard truth, or be vulnerable enough to apologize, or risk getting to know some-one really different. Or perhaps it will be the hard work of learning about the root causes of homelessness, and working in a soup kitchen. It may be the dangerous work of peacemaking in the Sudan or Palestine. It is all gospel work that leads to new life.

Awareness, vision, and hard work. Prayer and reconciliation. Call and response. We can use lots of different words, but they all are part of our challenge. You and I are called to change this world into something more like the reign of God. Are you ready to say yes?

The Family Table

Every fall, somehow, we survive another election season. Some of us rejoice and some of us grieve over the outcome, but by and large, we always demonstrate our ability as a nation to make a hard decision without resorting to bloodshed. The verbal rhetoric, however, comes pretty close. The ethics of electioneering sink ever lower, with clear examples of untruth and deceitful spin on both sides. And more distressing is the pervasiveness of religion and religious language in our elections. It seems especially striking that that heightened religious emphasis and such wretched ethical standards should coincide.

None of that is particularly saintly behavior, but it does seem to be characteristic of our culture at present. We have forgotten how to disagree without being disagreeable. We do it on the highways, in our churches, and across the globe. That's the bad news.

The good news is that you and I are heirs to a tradition that holds up a more creative vision.

When we worship, we ask God to knit us together into one communion and fellowship, to give us grace to follow the saints, so that we may know the joys for which we have been created. Joy is one of the fruits of being in communion and fellowship with each other, and it cannot be found outside of communion. Communion is not merely a gathering of like-minded folks who never disagree with each other. Communion is the scratchy proximity of near-enemies—not unlike the extended family gathered around the family table at Thanksgiving or Christmas or Grandma's birthday. Even if it is only a very small part of our being, it is our love for each other that brings us together around that table.

That vision of bringing a family together around the table underlies all of the biblical visions of the heavenly banquet and the kingdom of God. But it is a family that is far larger and more diverse and probably more exasperating than most of us can imagine. The writer of Revelation proclaims that 144,000 will be gathered for the banquet. It's a number that symbolizes eternal wholeness—a thousand times twelve times twelve. It is an image of those who love God, coming from each of the tribes of Israel. And then he turns around and sees an even greater multitude, coming from every nation and tradition, and in the time it was written, that meant every religious tradition. All the earth is gathering before the throne of God, not just the 144,000 out of the tribes of Israel. It is a joyful recognition of the communion of diverse peoples.

The saints and our loved ones are part of that crowd gathered before the throne of God. So too will be George Bush and John Kerry and a number of other people some of us would rather not sit next to at the table. If you and I are going to take seriously our vocation as saints, probably nothing is more important than the realization that it means living and working with the people around us and loving, yes loving, the people God puts in our way.

Being a saint, or living as one of the blessed, means recognizing that we can only approach God in the midst of that vast and mixed-up crowd. Being a saint means trusting that there is a gift somewhere under the grumpy exterior, whether it's ours or somebody else's. It also means we don't have to like somebody else in order to love that person.

Several years ago, I was on a flight into Las Vegas and seated next to me were a couple who'd just gotten married. Once we took off, one of the flight attendants came by and offered them a bottle of champagne and two glasses, saying, "Here's a gift from your friend, she wanted to congratulate you." They took what was offered and started a lively conversation with each other. Twenty minutes later, they were in the middle of an enormous fight. They weren't shouting, but pretty soon one glass of champagne was emptied in the other person's face. First one was crying, then the other. The words I overheard were about whether or not they should get divorced. They would stop talking for a few minutes and then one would lean over and twist the knife a little more. I was sitting there trying to read my book and not eavesdrop. Finally I got out a card and wrote on it the name of a book about conflict in relationships. The next time there was a lull in the fight I leaned over and said to them, "Believe it or not, marriage is about learning how to fight. But you have to learn how to fight fair. This book might be helpful."

Communion is about learning to live and thrive with those obnoxious people around us, whether they are in our homes, our churches, our nation, or around the globe. The communion of saints is our natural home, and it is the only place where true joy is to be found! We, too, need to learn how to fight fair and dignify our neighbors who stand with us before the throne of God. We will only learn to be fully present before that throne when we can see the fellow child of God in the odious person who stands next to us.

Live Long
and Prosper

Most of you have probably seen some episode of the *Star Trek* series and know that memorable opening line about boldly going where no one has gone before. In each episode, there's some sort of conflict between the crew of the starship and an alien menace, along with a parallel drama involving some of the crew members in their own conflict. That series was popular for many years, and its successors are still playing to good audiences, because they show us ourselves. Daily living brings us conflict, and it often seems like an encounter with a strange new world. Sometimes the people around us look a lot like aliens.

A couple of years ago at a House of Bishops meeting we heard from two speakers who invited us to consider the alien or "the other." The more moving of the two was Richard Rodriguez, a Pacific News Service editor, and the author of *Brown: The Last Discovery in America*. His thesis is that America is "brown" rather than black or white, both racially and in the way in which we relate to the other. The alien is contained within us, in our own distinct heritages, and not as "us" vs. "them." He pointed to his own heritage as a Mexican Indian Scots-Irish and reminded us that within himself he is both the conquistador and the conquered. At some deep level, he is expanding on what Pogo meant when he said, "We have met the enemy and he is us."

People of the Book, descendants of the three great Abrahamic faiths, talk about this encounter with the other in the language of each human being created in the image of God. God is found on the face of the alien, the other, just as much as God is found on our own faces. We, too, need boldness to go into that land of strangeness.

Human relationships are continual encounters with strange new worlds, seeking after the presence of God in the other. At times it seems like wandering in the desert, complaining about the food. Remember how the Israelites whined: "Oh, Moses, at least when we were slaves in Egypt we had leeks and melons and good meaty stews," or, "at least in the good old days we didn't have to work so hard." We all know the refrain.

There will come times in our relationships when some will be convinced that some of the rest are aliens, foreigners, strangers, or even just plain *weird*. There will be times filled with common rejoicing. And there will be lots of other times when our work and our lives feel pretty ordinary, as we just keep on keeping on. The times of rejoicing may not seem like they need a good deal of courage or boldness, but the other times will.

Boldness. Toni Cade Bambara calls it "sheer holy boldness" in *The Salt Eaters*. Boldness—strength and courage—is one of the principal fruits of our relationship with God. It comes from knowing and believing that we are loved beyond imagining. When we hear God call us "beloved" we begin to breathe in courage.

We all need boldness, strength, and courage in our life together. We may think we know what God wants of us, but getting agreement will take a dose of boldness and courage, and actually doing it will take a hefty portion. Sometimes it may take a real act of courage even to begin to imagine what God might be asking of us, for it will likely involve change. What does God ask of us, but to grow up into maturity, into the full stature of Christ, into the fullness of the people and community we were created to be? Yes, we are children of God, but we must also be adults of God, full partners in dreaming and building the reign of God.

Growing means change, and change takes courage. It is not a journey for cowards. But we never go alone. Jesus always sends the disciples out in groups. The gospel doesn't say, "Send out a laborer into the harvest." It's worded in the plural, for good reason. None of us is in this alone. Be of good courage, for we are all in this together, and God is our constant companion. That is cause for celebration.

But as Macrina Wiederkehr (a Roman Catholic Benedictine monastic) points out, "Celebration is not entertainment. It is deeper. It grows out of a strong conviction, a passion, that needs your response." In order to celebrate, we have to have full hearts and some passion about what we're up to. Can we celebrate? Will we enter into relationships with a passionate yearning to journey into strange new places together? Will we go boldly where we haven't been before?

It takes courage to celebrate. Jesus was called a glutton and a drunk because he continually invited people to God's party. The reign of God is all around us! How can you not rejoice? The harvest is plentiful, the groaning board is abundant, but the partygoers are few. Too few are willing to let go of their sure and certain security blankets and really enter into the dream God has for all creation. Rejoice!

Invitations to the celebration come every day. They come when we're in the desert complaining about the food—and God provides manna and quail, even when the wanderers turn up their noses. Invitations to celebrate come in the hospital room when your friend receives a terminal diagnosis. At least one of the invitations is about how to live an abundant life in the time that's left. There are a whole slew of invitations that come our way every day.

What would you like your community to look like five years from now? How will your community grow into a more abundant vision of the reign of God? How will it be the welcoming hands of God? Who needs to be invited? Dream boldly! Be of good courage! Think big and dream even bigger! God has surprising things in store, if you are willing to be courageous.

Be bold about proclaiming God's love for you and the people here, and God's dream for your own part of creation.

We are all saints. Let's live up to our name. My husband is fond of talking about the role of a teacher as a "guide on the side, rather than a sage on the stage." That's a fitting description of the role of clergy—they won't have all the answers, but they will challenge you to discover those answers in the midst of community.

We all share the job of boldly and courageously dreaming the dream God has for this place. It will be a challenge, and there will be times when it scares us to death, but God is always with us, and God is good, all the time.

Be courageous, take a friend to the vineyard with you, and find something to bless in the people you find the most alien. God's image is there to be discovered. Be bold, and give thanks in all things. God is with us, even in the strange land of promise called the reign of God.

Everybody in the Pool

❧

When I was a child, my brothers and sister and I had to eat everything on our plates, whether we liked it or not. I imagine it had something to do with the fact that my parents had grown up during the Depression, and lived through the scarcities of World War II. The one concession that was allowed was what we called the "dislike." We could name one food that we hated, and we could legally exclude that from our dinner. It didn't mean that my mother didn't cook it, just that we didn't have to eat it. There were various rules about how often you could change your "dislike," but it wasn't more than a couple of times a year. For years, my "dislike" bounced between eggplant and zucchini and spinach and winter squash. I'm still not very fond of winter squash, but these days I do relish the others.

Moses sounds a great deal like my parents must have felt, coping with a bunch of children who hate the food. "Eeuw! We hate this stuff! We want pizza, or hamburgers! At school we get good food!" Whine, whine, whine. I don't think any parent has ever avoided the food wars. And most parents cope with them by setting limits—"OK, you don't have to eat, but then you can't have anything else until the next meal," or something of the sort. And we praise the behavior we're after—when two-year-old Jill eats her carrots, we say, "Good girl." But children, being children, globalize that statement—kids soon begin to believe that following the rules means they are good, and not following the rules means they're bad. And if there isn't any counterbalance, before too long, children define themselves as Good or Bad, depending on how they cope with the rules in their lives.

That's exactly what's going on with Eldad and Medad and the seventy other prophets we read about in Numbers—the ones who do the expected and go out to the tent to do their prophesying get praised. But the ones who stay home and prophesy there can't be good because *they're not following the rules.* You can almost hear that boy who runs off to Moses to tattle—you can almost hear him shouting, "Not fair!" Jesus copes with the same kind of behavior from his disciples, too (Mark 9:38–43, 45, 47–48).

Those people aren't part of the club, so the disciples try to stop them from healing people.

That's a pretty common response, when you think about it. In the 2000 Olympics, the Romanian gymnast didn't follow the rules, so they took away her gold medal. Marian Jones' husband tested positive for something he wasn't supposed to, so people wanted to send him home, even though he wasn't competing. I'm not suggesting we throw out all the rules—they do a lot to level the playing field. But have you noticed how the rules have changed? Not too long ago, athletes who had received money that was in any way connected to sports couldn't compete in the Olympics. Now we have professional basketball and baseball players, and many if not most of the top Olympic athletes get paid for what they're doing. Rules are just rules, after all. Sometimes they change to fit the circumstances.

Our society is pretty concerned with rules. They're not always clear rules, but the people who are "in," the ones who have "made it," know what they are. We expect that if you work hard, you'll get ahead. And if you go to college, you can get a decent job. And if somebody is homeless, it's because he messed up in some way.

But you know what? The gospel doesn't work that way. The good news is that God loves us no matter what we do or don't do. We can't earn God's love by keeping all the rules. And we can't lose God's love by not keeping them. That sounds like bad news to some people—especially folks who think they do a pretty good job of keeping the rules.

Rules give us a way of defining ourselves in relation to the rest of the world.

They tell us who's in and who's out. They're a way of dividing up the world into "good people" and "bad people." But Jesus turns all that on its head. He basically says that we're all in, if we want to be. We're all sinners, because none of us can keep all the rules, but God loves us all nonetheless.

The main thing is knowing—deep down—how much we are loved. Most of us have a pretty tough time keeping the main thing the main thing. We tend to think that if we just keep the rules a little bit better that we'll be closer to God, or heaven, or loved better. Better than what? Better than whom?

In Mark the disciples complain about somebody who isn't part of the group doing something good. They're more worried about whether this guy has kept the rules first—they don't see that what's important is what he's doing. Was he baptized? Did he go to confession? Did he keep the Ten Commandments, or all 613 laws of the Torah? They want a credit check and a background check and letters from all his references first. They want to keep him out because they don't know if he's kept the rules or not.

And Jesus' response is one of the angriest in the gospels: "If you put a stumbling block in front of somebody who is looking for me," he says, "then maybe it's time for you to get some concrete overshoes." And then he says that keeping somebody out is like self-mutilation. And it is, of course. If we cut somebody off, we have cut off part of the body, part of God's body. Our hang-ups with rules encourage us to do just that. God's love transcends all our puny rules—even the rules in the Bible that we hold most dear. God loves the convicted murderer just as much as God loves you or me. Over and over and over again Jesus invites in the people that society's rules say should be kept out—public sinners, tax collectors, prostitutes, collaborators with the occupation government. If they're interested in coming to the feast, they're invited. Period.

Now think about those whom somebody would like to exclude. People of other races. Jesus says, you're invited, seat of honor. Children. Right up front. Folks with different physical or mental abilities. Ditto. The guy down the block who beats his children. If he wants to come, he's invited. Your sanctimonious Aunt Susie. Same thing. People who haven't been baptized. Ditto—down front. Muslims and Hindus, pagans and practicers of voodoo. You are loved as much as the next person, and you're invited to the feast, too.

Who's your favorite candidate for exclusion? I had somebody say to me once, if Hitler is in heaven, I don't want to go. Jesus' response, as to anyone else, would be, "You're invited, too." And people wonder why they crucified this sweet, gentle man.

Living an upright life, feeding the hungry, clothing the naked, healing the sick—that behavior comes from living in relationship with *love* itself, and only from that relationship. If we look around and see that kind of behavior—in others or in ourselves—then we know that person knows that he or she is well-loved.

We can't earn salvation, or God's love, or get into heaven by keeping the rules. We've already been invited, and the door's open—it's always open. The table is spread and the banquet's laid out, and we don't have to eat the eggplant if we don't want to. Though we may discover that trying a few bites might help us respect the feelings of our host, not to mention our fellow guests.

PART FIVE

DREAM A LITTLE DREAM

Opening Up
to the Vision of God

Dream a
Little Dream

Most of us have heard that tower of Babel story somewhere, maybe years and years ago, but is it just an old story? Those folks went out there on the plain of Shinar and started building a tower with the latest technology: fine, hard-baked brick and good sticky glue. Building a tower up to heaven, a tower higher than anyone had built before, a tower that would tell the entire earth how mighty they were.

Darwin taught us that evolutionary success is about being more successful than the ones in the next tribe over, and not just keeping up with the Joneses but outdoing them. The biblical story is all about human beings trying to compete in a different category—with God. Trying to control the divine, or the realm of Spirit, or storming heaven, is the heart of what the Bible calls sin. From Genesis to Revelation, the big story is about human beings trying to be God.

Babel is a new kind of social climbing. Storming heaven here means leaving the ground from which they were made—think about Adam and Eve, made of the earth. These tower builders are trying to escape their earthiness. Climbing up to heaven means they're not grounded anymore, they've forgotten or denied that they are creatures of the earth.

Having one language and the same words seems to be a big part of why God gets ticked off. The oneness the tower builders had wasn't the right kind. Even though they had a common language, they didn't use it appropriately. They wanted to be famous, get above themselves, or as my grandmother would have said, "They got too big for their britches." And the consequence of their hubris, of trying to leave their humanness behind, ends up dividing them, scattering them across the earth, and setting up renewed competition among them.

Lest we think this is just an old fairy tale, look where this story is set. In Hebrew, Shinar means the land of the two rivers, what was later called

Mesopotamia, and today is Iraq. We're still trying to build something there today, even if we disagree about just what kind of tower it might be.

Psalm 33 speaks pretty directly to our human attempts to find security in powerful people or military might, but the psalmist says God sees all the people of the earth—God who made them all, and the only ones who are happy are those who trust in God.

No, we won't find security in fortresses or armies or beating out the competition. Human beings will find peace only in the conscious presence of God, in the only place worthy of our hope.

Jesus is saying the same thing when he says, "If you're thirsty come to me and drink." He's echoing the prophet Jeremiah: "My people have forsaken me, the fountain of living water." The only source of life in the desert, the only sure refuge in time of despair, the only firm rock, the only answer to the deep sighs at midnight, the only adequate response to fear, is God.

But then Jesus goes on to say something even more striking: "Out of the believer's heart will come streams of living water." When you know where to find heaven—not in a tower or an army or anything else, but around you and among you and within you—then you can become that source of living water as well.

We have been given hope of becoming part of that fountain of living water. Baptism and confirmation are all about connecting to that artesian well of life, that bottomless spring, that geyser of God.

And when we're connected to that source, then we, too, can dream dreams and see visions of a world reconnected with God.

What dreams will you dream? What visions do you see? What sigh will the spirit make in you? Let go the dreams of a tower of power, and see how to be a fountain of life for the thirsty and fearful world all around.

What river of life will you be for the world around you?

What particular gifts do you bring? Are you a teacher, a water engineer, someone who likes to cook great feasts? Do you love sports? Anything that brings you joy, anything you would call your passion, can be a pipe that connects you to that geyser of God. Every single person has a passion like that, one that can be a source of living water for the world.

Will you work to restore the watercourses of this desert? Doing that right here could restore the fish populations of a dying lake and the people who have depended on them for generations.

Will you be water for those with no home to call their own? Will you cook for the hungry of our streets and those hidden in their homes? Will you be lifegiver for a lonely child or shut-in senior? Or for the immigrant who speaks another language? Will you use your athletic gifts to build a community of justice and peace? How is that water welling up in you going to slake the thirst of the world?

Dream! See! Your vision has something to do with the way you are made—that earthy, ordinary stuff of your life. Dig your toes into that sandy soil on the plains of Shinar. Look around at your neighbors. Who's thirsty? How will the water well out of you?

Be bold enough to dream of a world where all people speak a language of dignity and mutual respect. Bringing that dream to reality will not be easy, because you and I will have to help tear down those towers of power every day. We build them ourselves when we're not well-grounded in God. And the fearful around us build them higher every day.

Dream that dream, and put your own particular talents to work, and we will begin to see a river of peace.

Alternate Universe

My name is Katharine, and I'm a recovering scientist. I am still trying to understand the mysteries of creation in ways that don't demand physical evidence. I don't think I'm ever going to make it. Like Thomas and Mary and Martha and so many of the disciples, I want to see something before I can believe it. I got an inkling of another way of seeing when I watched a phenomenal program on *NOVA* about string theory. String theory is beginning to let physicists talk about the world of the atom and the world of galaxies in the same mathematical terms—something that hasn't been possible since Newton. It may be the grand unified theory that Einstein spent the last decades of his life looking for. I've had a warm place in my heart for theoretical physicists ever since I read some of the philosophical musings of Einstein, Heisenberg, and Bohr when I was in graduate school. They began to show me that even my fellow scientists saw the world as filled with mystery—and that maybe understanding the world doesn't always require sensory data. This *NOVA* program did a remarkable job of talking about string theory in a way that began to be understandable. One of the mathematical possibilities that comes along with string theory is a series of parallel universes—maybe something like what the author of Revelation means when he speaks of a new heaven, a new earth, and a new Jerusalem. We see how the world is around us, but that isn't all there is. The mystics and the prophets have always said that another world is possible. That's what the prophet Isaiah dreams about when he talks about feasts on the mountainside (Isa 25:6–9).

Physicists like Heisenberg have taught us that observing something in the quantum world changes reality—the observer has an effect on the system. Isaiah's vision of the heavenly banquet and the author of Revelation's dream of a new heaven and a new earth and the holy city of a new Jerusalem (Rev 21:1–6a) and Jesus' encounter with Lazarus' sisters, insisting that those who believe will see the glory of God (John 11:32–44), are saying the same thing. Being able to see something, even as a dream in your heart, begins to make that vision more possible. Isaiah's vision is God's dream for all of creation—people are well fed, no one mourns, and everyone is in right relationship. We can't begin to move toward that vision until we can see it. Revelation's author talks about the same thing—a new creation, where death holds no sway, where all things are new. The ability to see or imagine another possibility is intimately bound up in the whole of the good news. Jesus challenges Martha directly: "Didn't I tell you that if you believed, you would be able to see the glory of God?" We often think about believing as agreeing that an intellectual statement is true. Jesus is talking about belief as the vision in Martha's heart, what she gives her heart to (that's what "believe" really means—it's a variation on "belove" and the German *belieben*). Intellectual assent and beloving are vastly different things. Saints are those folks who have given their hearts to a vision like the dream of God. They're not the "holier-than-thou" sanctimonious goody-two-shoes of the distant past! Saints are folks like Peter, who sort of gets it some of the time, at least until he's confronted with mortal danger, and Martha, who knows her brother is so far gone he stinks by now. But both of them have a growing vision in their hearts that the world doesn't have to be the way they've always thought it was. That vision may not be fully visible all the time, but it's there. When we baptize people, we ask God to plant that vision in their hearts. And all of us agree to keep on tending it when it gets covered with rocks or choked by weeds. That vision looks a bit different in each one of us, but there are lots and lots of commonalities: death is never the last word. All people should be well-fed, no child should ever be abused.

I once heard a great interview on the radio show *Fresh Air*. Howard Tate's a blues musician who disappeared—just dropped out of sight—thirty years ago. The fellow who produced his music looked for him for years, until finally he gave him up for dead. And then, out of the blue, somebody he was talking to in Europe said she'd heard from Howard the day before. Howard had spent quite a few years on the street, addicted to this drug and that, until somebody reminded him that he was loved. He'd probably say he found Jesus again and his heart opened up enough to find that dream of God buried deep inside. He's sober, he's preaching, and he's making beautiful music again. Not just three days in the tomb, but thirty years, and he'd be the first to tell you he was stinking.

Every single person in Nevada has been touched by the ashes of dreams blown over the mountains from California. Those firestorms are horrible and awesome in their power. But next spring new growth will emerge from the blackened soil. The human devastation is harder to heal, but our prayers, our financial help to agencies like the Red Cross and Episcopal Relief and Development, and maybe even some physical assistance, will begin to help those people put their lives back together. The stories of neighbors helping strangers are already emerging. Our work is to find the corresponding vision in our own hearts—these, too, are our neighbors.

There is so much pain in this world, but what do we crazy Christians see? Promise. Alternative universes. Dreams and possibilities. Lazarus come back to life. Howard Tate's new album, *Rediscovered*. Children back at school in the fire-blackened hills. Saints are those crazy visionaries who say hello to death, and then greet what lies beyond it. Saints, however, are not so crazy that they fail to mourn the good part of God's creation that is gone in death. They do, and they shed tears abundant, and rail at God for making us mortal, but in the very scream they find God present with us, the God who suffers and dies with us, and points us to the new life that lies beyond.

What does that dream in your heart look like? The physicists may call it an alternative universe; we call it the dream of God. Pull it out, polish it off, and put it to work, because that vision can change the world.

Practicing Resurrection

You just never know what spring weather will bring, especially in the Nevada desert. I spent quite a bit of time traveling to far-flung parishes, and sometimes, getting there was a challenge. A couple of Aprils ago, I was faced with a dilemma—I had to get to a remote church for a visitation, but the long-term weather forecast was wretched—rain and snow and certainly not flyable conditions, at least for me. So I tried to get an airline seat, but everything on Southwest was sold out. So was America West. The only possibility was to go through Phoenix on a trip that took about eight hours and got in at one o'clock in the morning. The other alternative was to drive. So I kept watching the weather forecast, and it kept on saying snow and rain.

There was another complexity as well. I have to get re-certified to fly every two years, and I was overdue. It was incredibly windy all that week, and the only open slot I had was Friday morning. It turned out the instructor was available, and I figured I could do at least the ground instruction part of the review—it requires an hour of classroom and an hour of air time. Friday morning the wind was howling, and by the time I got to the airport it was blowing twenty-five with gusts over thirty knots. Ten minutes later, the tower said thirty knots, with gusts to thirty-nine. That was way more than I wanted to tackle, especially with the wind across the runway. We did our review in the classroom, and by then the wind had died down considerably. I wouldn't have gone up by myself, but it was a good opportunity to tackle something I didn't feel confident enough to handle alone.

The experience made me think of the apostle Thomas, widely maligned as the doubter. But I think I understand what he was going through. He wasn't going to believe the story his companions were telling until he experienced it, until his friend Jesus showed him how this resurrection thing worked.

Wendell Berry, the great environmentalist poet-theologian, has written a piece about somebody he calls a "mad farmer" who goes around shouting, "Practice resurrection!" "Practice resurrection." That's not bad advice. It's certainly what Thomas does—and maybe, just maybe, the other disciples are rehearsing the story and replaying the experience, too. Most of us don't "get it" the very first time. Most of us spend our lives learning what the reality of resurrection looks like, feels like, sounds like, and tastes like— because it keeps on happening in new ways every day of our lives.

How do we practice resurrection?

Maybe the most important skill is learning to live in the now, looking toward the future, rather than living in the past. That doesn't mean we forget about what's come before, though we are meant to honor what's good about it, and grieve what is gone if we need to. It also means that we live in hope for the new thing God is doing. It's the old issue of change— how many Episcopalians does it take to change a light bulb?[6]

I hope that we're learning to put a compact fluorescent bulb in there as soon as somebody notices that the old one isn't giving light anymore. If we're going to practice resurrection, we don't sit around whining about Thomas Edison spinning in his grave—"He never would have thought that was an adequate light bulb!"—or complaining that the old one was so much warmer (and dimmer), so now we have to look at the dirty walls. If we're going to practice resurrection, maybe we notice that repainting the walls means we can change the color, or it's an opportunity for the artists among us to paint a mural.

Resurrection means that creation isn't over and done with. And if we're made in the image of God, then we've got creation work to do. What's coming may not look exactly like what we knew before, but God promises that it will be abundant and life-giving.

Practicing resurrection means living in openness. It's a vulnerable atti- tude. Jesus invites Thomas to examine his wounds—come and see the ugliest thing you can imagine. God has made it a source of beauty and healing. It means that our fears, our inadequacies, the wretched parts of ourselves, can be the vehicle for new and more abundant life—if we're willing to confront them honestly and openly. In twelve-step programs, it's step number five—admitting what we've done wrong and doing our best to make amends. In the baptismal covenant, it's the second promise

6. Three: one to call the electrician, one to mix the martinis, and one to complain how much nicer the old light bulb was. Or, "Change?!?"

we make—to repent and return to the Lord. But it's not just our wrong-doing—the weak and untried parts of ourselves can be the stuff of new life, too. That's what exercise is all about—stressing, trying the weak parts of our bodies so that they become stronger. Our psyches and souls can find new strength too if we're willing to journey within and confront some of that darkness or fear or mystery. There's a remarkable phrase in Acts 3:19–20: "Repent therefore and turn to God so that your sins may be wiped out, so that times of refreshing may come from the presence of the Lord." Refreshment comes in the presence of God, and that presence is to be found even in the tomb and the depths of despair and the dark night of fear and abandonment—that is resurrection!

Practice resurrection. Live in open expectation of the new thing God is doing at all times and in all places. It means opening ourselves to that new thing, recognizing that the change it brings will cause some distress. But there is always more abundant life on the other side of the pain and grief that comes with change and growth.

I did make some embarrassing landings that Friday morning. But I also made some pretty good ones, and I learned a good bit in the process. And I did get to fly up to that parish after all. The challenging thing about flying—like living—is that you never learn everything. That is humbling, but it is also exhilarating.

Like Thomas, all of us get opportunities to learn something that we can't believe without firsthand experience. True joy and abundant life come out of those experiences of resurrection.

We have a remarkable opportunity to practice resurrection right now. In the aftermath of this war in Iraq, we can be emphatically open and vulnerable to something new. I don't know what it will look like—maybe you do—a sister city relationship between your home town and Nasiriyah? An exchange between peoples that might lead to greater understanding? A different way of conducting our foreign policy? We've already done some learning about how we've treated those who fought this war, whether we supported our government's policy or not. Most of the members of our Armed Forces know that people here have been praying for them. I don't think the Iraqi people know that yet. We have lots of opportunities to practice resurrection, even between those here who took opposing stands on this war. What can we learn from each other? How will you practice resurrection? Where will you find refreshment in the presence of God?

The Secret Places
of Your Heart

What do you dream of in the secret places of your heart? What wakes you up with longing in the middle of the night? Think about Solomon, renowned for his wisdom, awakened in the middle of the night to give answers to those questions. Most of us have experience with waking up to worry—about our health, that of our loved ones, or what our children are up to (especially the ones who still aren't home at two in the morning).

How often do we dream about what is or might be possible? In the face of those questions, Solomon asks for wisdom and understanding. What is it you yearn for?

Sometimes the seeds of those dreams are planted in us long before we are able to articulate an answer.

When I was a child of eight or nine, we lived in New Jersey, near Bell Labs, where my father worked. One evening my mother found me sitting on the curb watching the people who were walking home. When she asked me what I was doing, apparently I responded, "Looking for a wild-eyed mathematician." My father had talked about his colleagues in those terms, and I wanted to see what one looked like! I had forgotten about that incident until my mother reminded me, almost twenty years later, as I was getting ready to marry one.

When somebody asked me, early in my studies to be a priest, what my dream job would be, from somewhere deep inside came the answer, "Oh, I don't know—maybe being a circuit rider with an airplane." (Circuit riders were clerics, originally from the Methodist tradition, who traveled from church to church in rural areas to serve the sparse population.) Little did I know then that that would be a pretty good description of what I was called to do when I served as bishop in Nevada.

Those dreams became reality, albeit in unexpected ways, years and years after they first took root in me. You can probably tell similar stories.

Solomon asked for wisdom, and that was the one gift he needed more than any other, more than he knew, in trying to bring those robustly different tribal societies together to become one nation.

Jesus' parables about the kingdom of God are about the great dream that God dreams for all creation. A piece of that dream is planted in each one of us. All those examples—the mustard seed that produces a tree shrub to house the birds, the bit of yeast that leavens enough dough for a hundred loaves of bread, the hidden treasure and the fine pearl that searchers are willing to give all to possess, and the fishnet that gathers in all kinds of fish—all those images are pointing to the ways in which God's dream gathers substance.

That dream may surprise us when we least expect it, or we may find it by dint of hard looking. All sorts and conditions of people can find it— farmers, fishers, bakers, women, and men. It can require all of our substance to realize   we may have to "sell all" to acquire it. And God's dream gathers in the whole lot—the ones we judge good and the ones we judge bad—because the sorting doesn't come until the end of time, and it is not we who do it, but the angels.

What would those images be if Jesus had been walking around somewhere other than Palestine? Perhaps:

- the dream of God is like the prospector, burning up all his cash in order to find the mother lode
- the dream of God is like the child who quietly proclaims, "The Emperor has no clothes"
- the dream of God is like the family that scrimps all year to be able to afford a vacation in a corner of paradise
- the dream of God is like the quiet and not-so-quiet work of so many who strive to find peace and direction in a complex web of relationships.

God's dream is about using our own gifts—whatever they are—in full-bodied and earnest pursuit of that dream.

God's dream is about dreaming big dreams on behalf of the world— no more poverty, no more war, everyone fed and clothed and housed and educated.

God's dream is about being used up, giving all we have, in pursuit of that dream.

I heard a great story recently about going to sea. It's about a coast guard station, where new recruits come to learn the ropes—literally and figuratively—from the old salts who inhabit the place. The station's main function is old-fashioned lifesaving—responding to vessels in distress.

A monster storm blows up, and the young seaman begins to question the old mate.

"We don't really go out when the waves are this high, do we?

And a bit later: "We can't possibly go out when the barometer is that low."

The call comes in, and the mate begins to prepare the boat to launch out into the storm, and the crew continues, "How can we go out there when we can't be sure we'll ever come back?"

And finally the mate responds, "We don't have orders to come back."

Our piece of the dream is like that. We don't have orders to come back, either. The call of our wild is about spending all we have in search of that dream, whether it's making peace in our own families or across the globe. What part of that dream wakes you in the night? What are you willing to give to make it come to fruition?

What dream can you dream that is worth your all?

PART SIX
RECKLESS LOVE
Living Faith with Abandon

A New Thing

When I was a little girl, maybe six or seven, my grandmother promised to take me to Hawaii when I graduated from high school. She smoked and had developed emphysema, and her doctor told her to leave Seattle in the winters and go someplace warm. As a child, going to Hawaii seemed like a magical adventure. But my grandmother died three or four years later.

When our daughter Kate was only a couple of years old, my mother started talking about taking her to Europe when she graduated from high school. But my mother was in a plane crash soon after and was severely injured. After that, she didn't go anywhere by herself until she died.

I had largely forgotten about those conversations until Kate was in middle school. And then it came to me that there might be a way to find some new meaning in those old, unfulfilled promises. Kate and I sat down and talked, and decided that we would go to Hawaii together when she graduated from high school. We took that trip, and had a wonderful week together. We snorkeled, and went to the top of Mauna Kea, and lay on the beach, and read and talked. I brought home a couple of touristy souvenirs—a couple of starts for flowering ginger plants and a plumeria.

The plant starts were sort of soft, greenish-black sticks. The directions told how to plant them, but didn't say anything about how or when they would flower. I planted and I watered and I waited. The plumeria was a section of trunk, and you were supposed to plant it partway in the soil and partway sticking out. It started to shrivel up and rot after a few weeks, so I threw it out.

The ginger starts were a lot smaller, and got planted under several inches of soil. It got to be late fall and nothing was happening, so I dug down in one of the pots to see what was going on. It didn't seem to be rotting, but not much else was happening, either. I checked again a month later, and then again in January. I was getting sort of embarrassed by those empty pots sitting on my kitchen windowsill.

In February, one of them sent up a puny little green stalk not much bigger than a blade of grass. It grew incredibly slowly. A month later, there was another one in the same pot. Finally, two weeks later, the other barren pot produced a much larger and faster-growing spike that soon passed the other two.

Our lives are something like those plants. They are a series of dyings—promises that go unmet, and hopes that get buried and perhaps forgotten. Some of them shrivel and rot because conditions aren't right—maybe our friends or partners can't seem to meet us halfway, or one of us can't forgive the other, and the result is the end of a friendship, or a divorce. Sometimes all that's left of a great and flowering love is a dead-looking stump.

But those dyings can lead to new life. Sometimes those marriages and friendships have to die to old ways of relating to each other. Sometimes the death of a loved one leads to a new way of living and loving for the one who stays behind. Jesus is trying to tell his disciples that dying *is* the road to life, in *this* life.

Jesus says, "Those who love their life will lose it, and those who hate their life in this world will keep it for eternal life." That word "hate" is a troublesome one for us, but it also means "disregard," or "be indifferent to." Don't let your self-concern be the biggest thing in your life, or as *The Message*[7] puts it, "Let it go, be reckless in your love."

Be reckless in your love—that's what God does. Sow lots of seeds, keep on planting, even if a lot of them seem to die. Over and over again, God reaffirms the covenant with Israel, in spite of what those people do. God doesn't hang on to a list of misdeeds, God makes the covenant again and again with each new generation. God forgets what was done wrong, but God remembers the promise.

Reckless love. That's an incredible image! What would it mean for us to live like that? That's what Jesus does in the last moments of his earthly life—"Father, forgive them, for they don't know what they're doing." And on the cross, when he speaks to Mary and John, he says, "Woman behold your son, son your mother." Remember the love you share, and forget what's come between you.

Opportunities arise for all of us. How do we respond to people who disagree with us about war, or about the best course for our congrega-

---

7. Eugene Peterson, *The Message* (Colorado Springs: NavPress Publishing Group, 2002).

tion? Do we hang on to a memory of how that person has bruised us, or do we love recklessly? How do we meet a stranger who asks for help? Do we see a person who might endanger us, or a person who needs something we can offer?

That word, "reckless," means that we don't count or reckon the cost. It means to love, simply because that's what we've been created to do, without worrying about the consequences. God says to each one of us, you are my beloved, and you will continue to be my beloved, no matter what wretched thing you have done or not done. That's what Jeremiah is saying—God will keep on loving, when are you going to realize that? God keeps on scattering grains of wheat, even though not all of them grow into fruitful stalks. That is what God does so dramatically—and recklessly—in Jesus.

That kind of reckless loving means letting go of the hurts of the past, of what we have learned to expect from people based on past hurts. That is a kind of dying, but it is a dying for something greater. We let go of that limited expectation in order to embrace God's ongoing creation, for greater and more abundant life. Goethe put it this way, "As long as you have not comprehended this dying and becoming, you are but a shadowy guest upon this Earth." The Christian journey leads us into a hospital for shadowy guests, a way to learn how to die to old ways so that we can live abundantly.

That abundant life is ours for the asking, and the letting go. It's as close as our breath. The act of breathing is itself a small dying and invitation to new life. Letting go of our breath is a radical act of trust. It's a dying, but a dying for, so that we have room for a new breath.

Try this exercise. Close your eyes. Relax your body. Ease into your chair. As you breathe in, hear God saying to you, "I love you." As you let your breath go, focus on letting go with it something that binds you—an old hurt, a sin that's hard to forget, your frustration with your own or someone else's imperfection. As Jeremiah said, God has already forgotten it. God remembers only the promise. Even in the midst of our current global anxiety, God is doing a new thing.

All You Can Eat

Have you eaten fish recently? If I had my druthers, I wouldn't eat much of anything else. Several years ago, when I was on sabbatical, I visited a friend while I was driving around the West. I offered to take her out to dinner, and she suggested a sushi bar. They had an "all you can eat" deal that wasn't too exorbitant. I must have had twelve different kinds of fish—octopus and eel and tuna and salmon. I thought I'd died and gone to heaven. For me, having a meal of fish usually means celebration.

I've never quite understood why the Lenten tradition says eat fish, not meat, as a way of mortifying the flesh. For me, eating beef instead of fish would be penance. How do we square that tradition with fish as the primary food in Jesus' resurrection appearances? There's the one in John's gospel, where Jesus cooks a fish breakfast for some of the disciples after they've been out fishing all night.

Eating and feasting have always been a central image for what heaven is like, or the reign of God—when things are working right, when everyone has plenty to eat. If someone is hungry, then things are not as they should be. That's why the meal is so central to our tradition—both the meal at the altar and the meal in the parish hall. We are who we are because of what we eat, and because we eat together.

There's good historical evidence that the followers of Jesus ate together—their common meals were what held them together, and there's even evidence in Paul's letter to the Corinthians that it wasn't always a potluck. Some people came early, brought their own food, and had a party by themselves, while others went hungry.

There's also some tantalizing evidence that the early sacred meals included things besides bread and wine. An early eucharistic prayer by the third-century bishop and martyr Hippolytus has a blessing for cheese and fruit, besides wine and bread. And many scholars believe that fish was part of those early meals—probably because of the story in John's gospel, and the one about feeding the five thousand with bread and fish.

Why fish? It's certainly part of the normal diet in the part of Israel around the Sea of Galilee. But so are goat and sheep and even cheese. Several of the disciples were fishing when Jesus first called them. But others were collecting taxes and keeping public houses (bars).

Think about fishing. It's not like keeping cattle or growing potatoes— it's a much dicier proposition. The harvest comes as a completely unexpected gift. You can fish all day and all night and not catch a thing. You can't usually see what you're catching until the evidence is on the end of the line, or the net is straining at the winch. Fish are wild—even those bred in today's hatcheries or ocean pens are still pretty wild. They don't herd nicely like sheep with a dog. Fish are wild and uncontrollable and in many ways beyond our ken—something like God. Most of us know that the early Christians used the Greek word for fish, *ichthys*, as an acronym that meant Jesus Christ, son of God, savior—a secret sign from one believer to another. That's where the fish on bumpers came from, the ones who are often battling it out with Darwins.

The fishers who go down to the sea or the rivers go in eternal hopefulness, and they do their work in all sorts of weather, never knowing whether or not they will be successful. My father is fond of saying, "The fishing is always wonderful, and once in a while we catch something, too!" Fishing is what's important, not the contents of the creel at the end of the day. And it seems that companionship is a big part of what makes a successful fishing trip—whether it's you and a boatload of like-minded friends, or just you and the one who made Leviathan for the sport of it.

One of the most wonderful gifts I ever received was a fish. Several years ago, one of the men in the Spanish-speaking congregation I served showed up at my house on a Saturday afternoon with a great big salmon that he'd caught in a reservoir on the Santiam River in Oregon. It was totally unexpected. This was the gift of a man who worked three jobs to support his family, yet still took the time to go fishing—for the sport of it. Fishing was for him a sign of leisure, that he had some freedom in his life. And he wanted to share that with others. His name is Macario—which is what we translate as happy or blessed in the beatitudes.

Fish are a sign of abundance and blessing. That's one reason why people are so wrought up over the declining salmon and trout populations in the Northwest. We used to count our blessings by the size of the catch in Pyramid Lake, or the Truckee River. We can't do that anymore, but we are gaining a sense of how precious they are, even if it's only because they're so much rarer than they used to be.

Fish are probably an even better sign of resurrection than Easter eggs. (In my family, we usually eat salmon for Easter dinner!) Fish, like God, are wild and undomesticated. They're a sign of God's abundance. Everyone has an equal chance of catching a fish—it doesn't matter if you're homeless or a dotcom millionaire. God loves them all equally.

I have clergy friends who joke about the kind of insubstantial bread that's often used for communion—the kind that gave rise to the story about the archbishop who said, "It's one thing to believe this is the body of Christ, it's quite another to believe it's really bread." Sometimes we call that stuff "fish food." Maybe the originator of that term was really thinking about the kind of bread that some Baptists use—little flakes of wafer. But I think everybody missed something. This bread, no matter what it looks like, really is fish food—like the fish that Jesus shared with his disciples, it's a sign of new life, of God's overflowing abundance, and it's a reminder that God is always more, and more mysterious, than we can imagine. Anyone who's ever seen a salmon-spawning stream knows something about new life emerging from death. The stream may be filled with rotting carcasses, but there are countless thousands of eggs buried in the gravel, already developing into next season's fingerlings.

We are "witnesses of these things," the gospel tells us. To be a witness is to testify, to tell the story you know, what you've seen and heard and believe to be true. What story does sharing fish food lead you to tell? What stories can you tell about your experience of new life, and abundance, and the overwhelming love of God?

I'll bet you can tell some pretty good fish stories about the wild love of God working in your life. One of our duties as Christians is to tell one another the stories of our fishing trips. That is work we all share by virtue of our watery birth and baptism; we're all meant to go fishing and come back and tell the story—the old, old story—about the wild love of God.

Mother Love

Some of our mothers taught us what it was like to be loved. Some others of us grew up with mothers who couldn't really teach us much about love, because they'd never really learned themselves. We tend to idealize mothers as the perfect dispensers of love.

My own mother was dutiful and present when I was growing up, but she was never the warm, fuzzy type. Her own mother had been an active alcoholic for pretty significant chunks of my mother's childhood, and my mother never learned what it was like to be loved from her. When I was little, she was busy going to graduate school and taking care of the four of us children, and she didn't have a lot of extra time or energy. For a long time I thought my father was the one who really loved me, because he spent time teaching me to build radios, taking me backpacking, and joking at the dinner table.

But my mother gave me a great gift in the last part of her life. When she was in her early fifties, she was in a plane crash and suffered a severe head injury. She made a pretty good recovery over the next year, but then she started having grand mal seizures, and she couldn't live by herself any more. She lost most of what she valued about life—especially her intellectual capacity and her ability to be independent. She spent the next fourteen years of her life living in foster homes or institutions. She was angry and depressed for a lot of that time. But something happened in the last couple of years of her life. She found some peace, and she began to live life in thankfulness, in a way she'd never been able to do before. She delighted in very simple things—being in a group of people, weeding, putting plants in the ground, seeing the smile of a friend. She began to enjoy letting people do things for her. She learned to love in a way that she had never known before. In her vastly simplified life, she let go of being a martyr, she let go of believing that extravagant gifts were the only way to show love, and she learned to enjoy almost every minute of the day, for each instant held abundant gifts.

Some of our mothers did a better job than others. I believe that most of them did the best job they were capable of, whether they gave us idyllic childhoods or they fell short of what we might think is minimally functional mothering.

Sometimes mothers do their best work by getting out of the way, or by leaving. After all, children need that to grow up, too. After all, even Jesus gets out of the way so we can try his way for ourselves.

When Jesus is getting ready to leave his disciples, he begins to tell them good-bye. It's not so different from the speech a mother on her deathbed might give the kids: "Now children, I won't be with you much longer. You are going to keep looking for me . . . but you can't come where I'm going. I'm giving you some new instructions: love each other, just the way I've loved you. Everybody will know whose family you come from if you love each other."

The kids get a remarkable challenge—now it's time to put to work everything they've been taught. Love one another, as I have loved you.

It's an invitation to love in a way that doesn't repeat the foibles of our parents. And that's not a Hallmark sentiment. It's about blood, sweat, and tears. It's getting up in the middle of the night with a sick child, or taking bread to those who need a hand to get through the month on an inadequate food budget. It's visiting somebody in the hospital, someone who's afraid and alone. It's working hard to understand the position of someone who disagrees with you. It's promoting nonviolence in prison. It's the quiet kind of reaching out that cares for those in need in our congregations.

Love one another as I have loved you. Jesus feeds us with the very stuff of his body. At the Eucharist, the bread and wine nourish us—they strengthen backbones for that blood, sweat, and tears kind of loving.

We begin by feeding the physical hunger of the people around us. Jesus did so much of that that people called him a glutton and a drunk. A real party animal! But the feast feeds more than the stomach. Eating together and celebrating are about loving, and we can always expand the guest list. Jesus would probably ask, "Who isn't at the party?"

What does love look like? Getting out of the way, so another person can try. Blood, sweat, and tears. Feeding one another. Above all, love liberates, love sets us free to be more than we thought possible.

There are examples of that kind of love all around us—in our mothers and others, whether dutiful or earthy, proper or huggy. We can learn

something about loving from anyone who ever sets aside self-interest for
the sake of another. Only occasionally does loving have much to do with
warm fuzzies—it's a great deal more about making hard decisions that
lead to more abundant life.

In the same way that most adults learn to make peace with whatever
kind of parenting they got, whether it seemed adequate or not, a healthy
community learns how to love all its members, especially those on the
outside. William Temple, Archbishop of Canterbury in the 1940s, put it
well when he observed that the church is the only human institution that
exists primarily for the benefit of those outside of it. How does our love
draw the outsiders in?

Certainly some people are easier to love than others. Loving one
another doesn't mean we have to *like* everyone, but it does imply treating
everyone with dignity, looking for ways to liberate ourselves and others
for greater life, and it means continuing in relationship even when we disagree about almost everything. It also means continuing to expand the
guest list—looking for those who haven't enjoyed enough love. God
knows that's what's behind most forms of violence—people who live in
fear, who haven't known the kind of love that obliterates fear. Every school
shooting is the result of a person—or a few people— who feel excluded,
and devalued, and unloved. Every human separation, war, aggression,
even road rage, is about the absence of love. The abuse of prisoners in Iraq
is about people exerting their authority in humiliating the powerless
because they don't know how abundantly they or their enemies are loved.

Sometimes love requires letting go and moving on, so that we or the
other can grow. That often feels like the hardest sort of loving, for it can
come across as rejection. Think about those disciples standing around on
Easter, feeling abandoned. In the midst of their fear and resistance, what
does Jesus say?

Love one another as I have loved you. Befriend the stranger. Engage
your enemy in love. Challenge the unlovable. Go hunting for the unloved.

When we know the love that bursts the doors of tombs, when we insist
and expect to find new life in the darkest and most difficult of days, we
can reach beyond whatever divides us. Love one another as God loves
us—like the most challenging and nurturing of parents, absent and present, male and female, and beyond the limits of all human understanding.

PART SEVEN

GOD & ME
Finding a Personal Path

Gone Fishin'

Twenty to twenty-five years ago I spent a lot of time fishing with big nets, towing them around behind big ships, hunting for squid, more often catching lots of fish. You learn right away that you can get into trouble pretty quickly if you're too successful. Ship captains, whether they're driving fishing boats or research vessels, get really nervous when they're asked to tow big weights around. The most dangerous moments at sea come when you've got a big load at the end of the wire. When it's still a hundred fathoms down in a heaving sea, the weight of that net puts immense strain on the winches and the wire and all of the ship's fabric. And while that load is whipping around above the waves as you try to get it back aboard, there's the constant danger of having everybody on deck squashed or swept overboard.

Fishing is a dangerous business, whether you're after fish, or squid, or people. And it's the abundance that scares us. Nobody wants to catch too much—we don't want to sink the boat (or even rock it), we don't want to exceed our salmon quota, we don't want a big load of trash fish. I imagine we'd be awfully nervous if the pews were suddenly so full it was hard to find our accustomed seat.

Jesus wanders onto Simon's boat and tells him where to fish. Simon has worked all night and not caught a thing, "No fish out there, Rabbi." But he relents, goes out into deeper water, gives it his best, and surprise! The catch of the decade.

Simon gets what he's always dreamed of, and more, and his reaction is terror.

There's truth in what they say: Be careful what you pray for—you might get it.

But that is how God fishes for us. God blesses us with abundance, wherever we are, once we learn how to see it. Somehow, though, I think God uses a lure more often than a net. Desire and attraction and hunger and hope are all in God's bait bucket. If we're going to join this divine fishing expedition, we soon discover that dancing in the aisles is more likely to catch someone than Saturday morning door-knocking with tracts. And a beckoning wave and a wink or a hug are likelier bait than finger-shaking. Because this fishing trip has abundant life as its grand goal, not punishment or death or destruction.

Abundant life. That's still pretty scary for most of us. Abundant life comes from relying on what is most important—as that amateur fishing guide reminds us. (Did you know that "amateur" means one who loves what s/he does?)

Jesus tells Peter to let the net down into deep water. For most of us, "deep water" means a place to get into trouble, a place of danger. But think about it—deep water, wide-open sea, depths of the ocean, "ocean depth of happy rest"—they're all images of the divine source of creation. The source of abundance, and maybe terror, too, even when we recognize it for what it is.

What is it that frightens us so about God's abundant blessing? The fact that we can't control it, or produce it ourselves? That seems to be at least part of what troubles both Simon Peter and Gideon: "This is beyond my doing," Peter protests. That abundant blessing is purely and simply *gift*, and we can't earn it or deserve it or bottle it up to put on the shelf. Like the air we breathe, it is all around us, even when we don't notice it. Those fish were there, even when Simon Peter hadn't seen a single one of them. On that particular day, the great catch was given to Peter and James and John. It didn't go to Matthias or Barnabas or Paul. The story doesn't tell us what happened to all those fish, but I think it's safe to assume that they got eaten by hungry people or went to fertilize some farmer's fields. Somehow, that gift got shared.

Some of us are terrified by abundance because we rightly recognize that some response is expected, and it might be more than sending a thank-you note. How can we keep from singing—and dancing, and rejoicing—when we begin to see the bounty all around us? Once we recognize that outrageous abundance, it begins to pull us out of our usual way of being, and life isn't going to be the same old, same old, anymore. Anyone who's ever won the lottery, or received an unexpected inheritance, can tell you that life changes. Running smack into that big catch sends Simon off in a completely new direction, and even gives him a new name. Life's been turned upside down, and as G. K. Chesterton used to say of St.

Francis, now he sees the world hanging from God's graciousness, depending on God, rather than sitting fixed and immovable on its ancient foundations. Now it's time to "be thankful God hasn't dropped the whole cosmos like a vast crystal to be shattered into falling stars."

Sometimes the abundance terrifies because we don't recognize the blessing. Peter's initial reaction was at some level about self-preservation. "Uh-oh, now I'm really in deep water." He was afraid he would die, because his tradition told him you couldn't look on the face of God and live. It was an awesome, or maybe an awe full experience. Learning you have a terminal illness is like that. It is filled with blessings, but you have to learn to look for them. Knowing, at least approximately, the length of our days can give an urgency and immediacy to life, a zest even, that most of us miss most of the time. Some of the most alive people I've known were actively dying, because they knew the preciousness of each moment, and were out there fishing for every blessing they could find. When's the last time you went fishing for blessings?

Jesus is really saying to Peter that he will become the net, or part of it, as he goes off to fish in other seas. We all make up that net, interconnected, tied together, sometimes torn, setting out—and sent out—to fish for life. We fish wherever we are, whatever we're doing. The people we love become part of the net. And the net grows and deepens, and sweeps ever more blessings from that rich and fertile sea of life.

We go fishing as part of the net every day of our lives. What we catch depends on grace and the gift of awareness. Some of the fish out there are so small that all we may see is a brief flash of light as they pass through the net. One brief encounter may be our only chance to know that particular blessing. The art of this kind of fishing is to keep our eyes open to embrace those brief flashes.

I have been caught in a great net of abundance the times I've had to leave one place and move on to another. Saying good-bye is a painful kind of abundance, but it's also been filled with blessing, as people have told me of the deep connections in our web of relationships, and as I've watched new and lively leadership emerge. That's not to say that it doesn't hurt to have the net stretched quite this far. It does hurt. But we're all being reminded of the wider abundance of these deep waters. We know that this net reaches to faraway places. The net of our communities will be stretched beyond our comfort, or maybe even torn, but those gaps and strains will be opportunities for growth, and space for others to join the fishing.

Our response to this abundance is to give thanks, and rejoice, and keep on fishing.

How are we going to respond, today, and tomorrow, when we meet the next terror? Can we remember to ask, "Where is the blessing in this encounter? In this difficult person?" Can we remember to go fishing when the next challenge looms? Can we remember that abundant life is to be found there?

The next time terror or pain or grief strikes, fear not: go fishing!

Come to the Feast

I love to hike, and whenever I get the chance, I spend my day off in the mountains, and my husband and I often spend part of our vacation back-packing. When I go hiking for the day, I usually take the same thing for lunch—a can of kippered herring, some crackers, and whatever else I can find—cookies, carrots, an apple. But the kippers and crackers are a con-stant. Once in a while I'll take a can of sardines. There's something about bread and fish in the wilderness that still satisfies.

The meals of the early Christians probably included fish, and fruit and cheese, as well as bread and wine. The holy meal didn't get pared down to bread and wine until later, but even that more limited meal was intended to signify the great banquet, the vast, overflowing abundance of God—even when things looked bad. Consider the sorrow of Jesus mourning for John the Baptist, who's just been murdered by Herod. But the cries of those in need pull him away, remind him there is more than grief in this place. God's abundance won't stop with mourning.

The disciples, meanwhile, are feeling pretty nervous, even helpless, so they ask Jesus to send folks away to scrounge for their dinners. What's this mob going to do when they get *really* hungry? But Jesus tells them to feed the crowd themselves. Their response: "Oh no, we don't have enough—only five loaves of bread and two little fish!"

About fifteen years ago, I was senior warden in my parish. The rector convinced me to serve a second year as senior warden, and then he resigned. I was not amused. The parish was hurting—the people who had given the rector a hard time were in one camp, and the ones who were mad about the rector leaving were in another, and there were a bunch of other folks who were just plain ticked off that we all couldn't seem to get along. We got an interim priest within a couple of months.

Father Eng arrived in our midst, and began to tell us stories about the discrimination he'd suffered growing up Chinese in Seattle. And he put us to work. For Lent that year, he offered everybody in the parish five dollars and asked us to do something with that five dollars during Lent and bring the profit back at Easter. A couple of little girls bought barrettes and ribbons and sold fancy hair decorations to their friends. Several people baked bread, or cookies, or made dried soup mix and sold it. One fellow paid for developing some of the slides from his Mt. McKinley climb, had a slide show, took up a collection, and made over a hundred dollars. The high school kids bought soap and a hose and washed cars all spring (in Oregon most of the year there's often reason to wash the same car every other day). I know there were a few doubters—people who stood aloof because they didn't believe that five dollars could make any difference at all. At the end of Lent we had collected several thousand dollars, which was given to some good cause, but more importantly, we'd forgotten what we'd been fighting about. We discovered that there was an incredible abundance right there in the midst of the people we disagreed with.

The disciples were worried because there wasn't enough food to go around. They didn't want a riot on their hands. We get anxious, too, when we see scarcity, and that's what leads to intense conflict. If there's only one way to see the world, then my way had better be it! If there's not enough water, or food, or living space, then our instincts lead us to defend what we do have. But when we can live out of an attitude of abundance, the urge to be defensive, or aggressive, or anxious, or selfish goes way down.

That's what Paul says in his letter to the Romans. Nothing can separate us from the abundant love of God—absolutely nothing, not armed conflict, not death or illness, nothing can get in the way of that divine abundance. When we can see the world through the lens of abundance, nothing can ruffle our feathers. That is what the peace of God is all about—resting in the sure and certain confidence that there's more to this life than we see at the moment, that God is already doing a new thing even in the midst of the most awful event we can imagine, and that the love of God is at work—just like thousands of people being fed with a lunch that looks like it's barely enough for two.

All over the place, parish food closets and soup kitchens feed more people than anybody has any right to expect. The labor of a few people and the gifts of more mean that a surprising number of hungry people get fed every day, even in the midst of enormous obstacles. Any one of those volunteers, or even all of them, could have thrown up their hands and said, "This is impossible. We can't feed people under these conditions." But they were sure that more was going on than the obstacles.

So, what are the impossible situations in your life? Relationships gone awry? Financial pressures? Children—or parents—who won't act like they should? One too many things to fix?

What do we see, scarcity or abundance?

My airplane mechanic went out of business a few weeks ago. Shortly after that, a piece on the plane's nose gear broke. The airport here doesn't have any other mechanics able to do the work. It's been an enormous hassle, and it's not finished yet. A week later my laptop died while I was on the road. It was dead, dead, dead, and I couldn't even get any data off the hard drive. No resurrection for *that* computer! So where was the abundance for me that week? It wasn't always easy to see it, but there were glimmers: I had to drive to Reno instead of flying, and spent some wonderful hours on the road with my husband. We came back on a back road and visited an ichthyosaur dig I would never have seen if I'd flown. I remembered that there were worse things than being out of e-mail contact with the world— the spam artists couldn't find me thirteen times a day! And I ended up knowing a whole lot more about airplane repairs than I did before.

Where is the abundance in your life, in your community? There is a feast all around us. All we have to do is look, and taste, and expect to find it. It's a mountainous abundance, full measure, pressed down, and overflowing. It doesn't take much to remind us— maybe just a snack in the wilderness, just some crackers and herring, just a bit of bread and wine. Come to the feast!

Letting Go

❖

Sometimes the comic strip *Sally Forth* nails our humanity. Here's one of my favorites: The husband has gotten a new video camera, and he's sticking the lens into every possible moment in the family's life. The daughter has put "KEEP OUT" signs on her door; the wife has to chase him out of the bathroom when she's taking a shower; and everybody is getting royally annoyed.

We live in a society that seems to pay a lot of attention to preserving memories—think about the industry built up around taking pictures, and now we have video cameras, and digital cameras, and tape recorders. I've seen ads recently for classes that will teach you how to build memory-boxes, or put together scrapbooks.

What would you take with you if you had to evacuate your house with five minutes' notice? Photo albums and legal documents seem to be what people most often mention.

What is so important to us about the past? Why do we try to hang on to it so tightly?

The prophet Isaiah, though, tells the people, "Do not remember the former things, or consider the things of old" (Isa 43:18). The great exodus from Egypt, that great and wonderful tale of delivery—how can Israel forget that? But God seems to be saying, "Forget about the past, for I am doing a new thing—don't you see it?" (Phil 3:13). Paul talks about letting go of the past as well: "This one thing I do: forgetting what lies behind and straining forward to what lies ahead."

What kind of letting go are they talking about? Why should Israel forget about the exodus? It seems to have more to do with perspective, with focusing on the new thing, and what lies ahead, rather than on the past. There is something about an attitude that focuses on the past that keeps us from recognizing the new thing that is happening all around us.

If I have an image in my head of a little boy at age three, it's going to be very difficult for me to appreciate who he is at age six. My expectations color what I see. If my relationship with someone is focused on what she did to offend me three years ago, I'm going to have a really hard time greeting her with any kind of openness. If my self-image is based on having some disease, then that's going to shape and limit who or what I can be in the future.

Something closer to home: if our understanding of church is based solely on what it's been in the past, then how will we be able to grow and change as the culture changes and those who come to join us change? The idea isn't to give up every good memory or every good influence from the past, but not to let the past define who or what you are now, or who you might become. Isaiah is saying to Israel, "The exodus was great and wonderful, but God continues to deliver you. The passage through the Red Sea wasn't your defining moment—you continue to have a relationship with God."

New things aren't always so easy to accept. Consider the parable of the vineyard. Our natural tendency is to identify with the tenants of the vineyard. They're rebelling because things are changing. They're being asked to share the produce with the landlord. But it seems like life has gone on for a long time without any account being asked, and now they resent the change, even though they knew it would come eventually. So they try to maintain the status quo by beating up the bill collectors. Finally they kill the heir. Forget the past, even if it was a liberating act, like getting out of Egypt, or receiving a vineyard to tend. Listen and watch for the new thing. The future is not going to look like the past.

Those messengers from the landlord are fascinating figures. I wonder how many messengers of change we beat up and throw out, because we don't want to hear the message. I have the sense that they are all around us, and it's probably not too hard to recognize them for who they are. If they bring a message that sounds like Jesus, we can probably trust that they're the real thing. If they call us to fruitfulness, if they call us to love our neighbor as ourselves, they've probably come from the landlord.

"The stone that the builders rejected has become the cornerstone." The new building is being constructed out of the rejects of the last building. Who or what has been rejected from your building? Who doesn't fit the picture? Look well, for the rejected is probably of God.

Think about the parts of ourselves we are least willing to acknowledge—that part of us that seems most wayward, most sinful. Maybe it's a habit of shading the truth, or maybe we have a hard time remembering whose vineyard we're living in. Maybe it's that part of ourselves we think is least forgivable. But that part of ourselves is our greatest opportunity for relationship with God—that wound, if you will, has the most potential for healing. But nothing's going to happen until we can begin to let go of its defining nature. In some sense, we can't see the new thing God is working in us until we stop expecting this wound to define our future.

If we look for it, we can see new life springing up everywhere. None of us, I think, really wants to hang on to the dead past of winter. Why do we hang on to the past of our lives? What new thing is God doing in your life and in mine, if we will only notice?

Unceasing Prayer

What is it we ask of God? Most of our prayers are usually for people we know and care about; they're prayers for healing or comfort.

What is your unceasing prayer? A longstanding one of mine is for peace—in the Middle East, in Afghanistan, in Ireland and Africa, and in all those areas of strife around the globe.

What is the undying prayer of your heart? It may be that the most central, the most often prayed dream of our collective Christian heart is for the reign of God to come on earth—your kingdom come, O Lord. The reign of God on earth is a community at peace, a city where justice is the rule of the day, a place in our midst where prejudice has vanished, where the diverse gifts with which we have been so abundantly blessed are equally valued.

Jesus charges his disciples to ask God for what is in keeping with what he has taught us. Ask in the name of the holy human one, and he will most certainly give it to you. Ask and you will receive. Ask and your joy will be complete. As *The Message* puts it, "Your joy will be like a river overflowing its banks."

That river imagery is highly appropriate, like the flowing river of peace we sing about, and like the river of life in which each of us was washed and made new. Our baptism was invitation into that dream of God, that dream of shalom.

Each of us was commissioned in that river, together sent as the Body of Christ to be and do the reign of God both here and wherever we live and move and have our being. That watery death was an invitation, a call to leadership in this divine endeavor. We've all been commissioned as ministers of God's government, each with unique portfolio. Some are ministers of education. Some are ministers of health. Others are ministers of childcare, or sanitation, or ecosystem management. The platform of this government for which we labor is simple—the reign of God incarnate, the reign of God made real. Ask, and your joy will overflow. Dream big, dare to ask outrageous things, and get ready to be surprised!

Sitting on the Columbia River in southern Washington State is St. James Church, in an old town called Cathlamet. It's a tired and depressed town, long dependent on the fishing industry, on logging, and on dairying. Fifteen years ago, the bottom began to fall out of all of those means of livelihood. Suddenly almost all the wage earners in the community were without employment. One of the twelve or fifteen members of St. James' looked around and noticed that the women in the community were having to find employment after years of raising children. There was no childcare available in the community, and she asked the vestry for permission to use the two Sunday school classrooms. If she could find seven children, she proposed, the parish could break even, and make a small difference in Cathlamet. The vestry agreed, and she began. Ten years later, the St. James Family Center provides childcare, after-school programs, parenting classes, teen outreach, meeting space for the community, and manages the county domestic violence shelter. It has long since outgrown those two Sunday school rooms and is housed in a big blue barn of a building that sits on land the congregation was saving to build a proper sanctuary. The Family Center operates on a budget of three quarters of a million dollars and is the county's third largest employer. The congregation is still under twenty people on Sunday, but they have fostered a remarkable instance of the reign of God in that part of Washington. That congregation has remarkably clear leadership, from each member of their vestry, from their local priest and deacon, and from every baptized person in that congregation. They understand that they exist as enablers of God's dream, and they are willing to use every resource at hand to build that dream.

What is the dream of your heart? Are you willing to ask? Are you willing to storm the doors of heaven in search of that dream?

Again I recall the story that says when each of us comes to the day of judgment, Moses will ask us if we've enjoyed everything God gave us to enjoy. I think I've always heard that to mean that we're meant to live in such a way that the abundance of God's gifts does not escape us, that we're meant to marvel at the wonders of all creation, and that we're meant to glory in God's profligate love. But I wonder if perhaps it does not mean that joy is made real in dreaming and asking.

What is the deep prayer of your heart? How is that dream becoming flesh? Ask, demand, insist that that dream be accomplished. Ask, and your joy will begin to overflow like the banks of a river in flood. Ask, and your joy will be full and deep and wide as the limits of God's love.

Paying Attention

Let's consider the ministry of paying attention—or "showing up." In another age it probably would have been called obedience, but we've forgotten that that word originally meant listening. Listening is about being open to hearing the voice of God, to discerning the subtle invitations of the Spirit. Benedict in his Rule speaks of listening with the ear of your heart.

A couple of examples. One Friday I was sitting in the office trying to plow through the mountain of mail that had accumulated while I'd been away. The phone rang and I answered it to find that a young man wanted money for a bus ticket. I referred him to the deacon at the church next door to my office. He was a bit pushy, telling me that he had called there earlier and no one answered. I assured him that the office was open till 4 p.m. One minute later he called back—no, the deacon isn't in, and the church gives all their money to the feeding program. I really didn't want to deal with this situation—it was clear that I was going to have to go down to the bus station and deal with it in person. The man began telling me his story, and his companion kept inserting information, so he'd have to stop talking to listen to her, and then repeat it to me, all the while conversing on a cell phone and walking along a busy street. They seemed to have done their homework—they knew how much the tickets were going to cost and that a charity discount could be had if the donor were a religious agency. And then the message got passed along that the woman had been baptized in an Episcopal church in Washington. OK, I said, I'll meet you at the bus station. It was a grace-filled experience for me. We got their bus tickets, and as I was leaving they told me they were hungry, so we went off to one of the downtown buffets and got them tickets there as well.

This is one of the blessings of Las Vegas: as much as you want to eat for a very reasonable price, as long as you don't mind walking through the casino. It turned out that they had come to Las Vegas looking for work and spent all their cash for two nights in a hotel. They could not find any work, but discovered that the man's grandfather would rent them a trailer if they could get to Texas. This young man was just out of the army, but there isn't much civilian demand for artillery radar operators. His wife was six months pregnant. It's a story that is repeated in Las Vegas more often than you would imagine, but for me it was an opportunity to hear, to really listen, to the story of two Christs on the streets of Las Vegas.

One more example. I was up in the Reno office and got a call from one of the diocesan officers who was trying to track down the archdeacon. He'd gotten a call requesting a hospital visit for a Paiute woman who was very ill. The archdeacon's phone had been busy for hours, so I said I would send him an e-mail. In the e-mail I offered to go if he couldn't, but I told him that I wouldn't be available until that evening. Well, I finished out the day's appointments and meetings, went off to my hotel room, changed into my blue jeans, and sat down to do my e-mail and relax. And there in my e-mail was a note from the archdeacon saying he couldn't go that day and would I please show up in his stead. It was 8:30 at night, and I did not really want to put my duds back on and go off to find this woman I'd never met. But at least I knew where the hospital was. I found the right wing of the hospital and asked to see the woman, only to be told that she was having a procedure and I would have to wait. I looked around in the waiting room and spied one face I recognized. She introduced me to the twenty or so relatives waiting there, and we had a prayer together and began to hear stories about Adeline. It was an incredibly grace-filled hour, and then a couple of us were able to go in and pray with her in person. She was at peace, knew that death was near, and was ready for whatever the next hours and days would bring. Her concern was only for her family. I went back to my hotel richly blessed by the meeting.

Listening is an attitude of openness and vulnerability. If we're really paying attention, it means we're willing to hear something other that what we expect. I don't know about you, but I don't do it perfectly. I often think I have a pretty clear idea of what ought to happen—which usually means I'm not as able to hear something different.

When was the last time you let God surprise you? The ability to surprise us may be the most telling characteristic of the divine. If we really believe that God is more than we can imagine, then of course we should expect to be surprised!

But we don't always receive that surprise with open arms—at least I don't. I greatly enjoyed my life as an oceanographer. I loved going to sea, I loved working on squids and octopuses—I thought I had the most fascinating job in the world. And then the bottom fell out of the federal research budget in the mid-1980s. I couldn't find a job from Hawaii to Washington, D.C. I became the recipient of countless letters that went something like, "You are one of 125 well-qualified applicants . . ." My only hope for staying in oceanography was to spend all my time writing grant proposals—which no one seemed to be funding anyway.

Right at the same time, three people in my congregation asked me if I'd ever thought about ordination. I was shocked! It wasn't something little girls aspired to when I was growing up, and I just couldn't see how it could make sense. But it was a strange enough experience that I went and talked to the rector about it at some length. We came to the conclusion that at the very least the timing wasn't right. For one, my husband thought it was the craziest thing he'd ever heard of. So I went off and looked for other things to do. I got involved in the community and helped to start a chapter of Habitat for Humanity. I served as treasurer of a women's philanthropic organization in town. I chaired the parent organization at my daughter's school. I took a number of courses in the religious studies department at Oregon State. And then I was asked to teach some of those courses. Then I was asked to preach in my home parish, right before the first Gulf War started. We were scheduled to have morning prayer, because all the clergy were to be away at Diocesan Convention. Well, the experience of preaching, of preparing to do it, and the feedback I got afterward, finally let me hear the surprising thing people in the congregation were asking of me. I was in seminary six months later. The humorous part to me now is that I can still recall the time I had to give my first in-class presentation in graduate school. I was so terrified that I hardly slept a wink the night before!

A few years ago, I spent a couple of months traveling around the western dioceses that are engaged in some form of total ministry—what in some places is called shared or mutual ministry. I wanted to see what it looked like in different places, and what made for success, because I was working with a task force in the Diocese of Oregon that was trying to encourage that way of being church for congregations both large and small. I went over to eastern Oregon, up into the Yakima Valley, down into northern California, into Nevada, Colorado, Wyoming, Utah, and Idaho. I discovered that the vital congregations, the ones that really succeeded in living out a baptismal vision of ministry, were the ones that had paid attention to the needs of their communities. They had a reason for existence that transcended Sunday morning. Their ministries from Monday through Saturday flowed out of their Sunday morning experience—indeed their ministries overflowed the walls of the church. The common thread was how well these congregations *listened*. Otherwise, these congregations were incredibly varied—one of them spoke Spanish; a few were pretty high church; some had paid staff. They had feeding ministries, English as a Second Language and immigrant assistance programs, some focused on the needs of young people and some on the elderly. But all of them were engaged in transforming their communities, because they had listened and heard.

A couple of weeks before I set off on that journey around the dioceses of the West, I was meeting with my clergy support group in Oregon, and the deployment officer piped up out of the blue and said, "Is any of you interested in running for bishop in Florida or Nevada?" We all guffawed and went on talking about the challenges in our various places of ministry. I continued with my plans for sabbatical and went off to interview congregations.

A month or so later I came to the church in Sparks, Nevada, right before Lent started. That congregation has a remarkable after-school program that serves low-income latchkey children in the neighborhood—with a meal, help with homework, games, and activities. I had a series of great interviews with folks in the church, ate pancakes with them on Shrove Tuesday, and joined the rector for the midday Ash Wednesday service. As I was packing up to continue my journey, she said to me, "What you've done here is an awful lot like a bishop's visit. You should let your name be submitted in this election process." Well, I thought that was just downright ridiculous and I told her so.

But as I drove all those hundreds of miles over the next few weeks, that question wouldn't let me go. Maybe we really shouldn't start Lent fasting—maybe it does something to our brains. By the time I got home, I realized that even as terrifying an idea as it seemed, this was something I was supposed to listen to. I had no idea where it would lead, but I knew I was supposed to say yes.

The spiritual journey is about learning to listen. Even when we'd rather not. Even when we're terrified, or convinced that we know we're going to do something else.

I think maybe one of the Benedictines put it this way: the spiritual task is to show up, pay attention, tell the truth, and leave the results to God. That really is what this crazy journey is all about. I like that aphorism almost as much as the one the monks taught me my first year in seminary, "It's much easier to ask forgiveness than it is to get permission." That way of looking at the world grows out of a passion to answer the godly call of the moment, rather than worrying about how it's going to look, or what other folks are going to say, or what canon you're going to violate. (You didn't hear me say that.) Answering with action, when we've really listened, is going to take us down some very surprising paths.

Where is God trying to surprise you into a new way of looking at the world, or your neighbor, or your own vocation?

Be assured that God *is* trying to surprise us. As Rabbi Kirschner says, to do theology—to live the spiritual life—without a sense of humor is blasphemy. If it is of God, the unexpected will be part of it.

Now, where is God asking you to show up? What is God asking you to pay attention to?

Bearing Our Crosses

Who or what is your cross to bear? Your spouse? Child? Parent? Boss? That's how we often hear those words of Jesus, "Take up your cross and follow me." We think they mean the person or the problem in our lives that bugs us the most. As in, "My mother-in-law is just my cross to bear!" And if we do it theatrically enough, somebody may say to us, "Oh get down off that cross, someone else needs the wood!" That kind of thinking is wrapped up with the sense that we're supposed to suffer in this life, and that to be an especially holy person means going looking for things to suffer over. While most of us can recognize that life does bring suffering, and a lot of it seems undeserved, Jesus also said that he had something to do with abundant life. Our tradition and our experience often remind us that sometimes life is more abundant because of the way we cope with the suffering that life gives us. But abundant life doesn't have anything to do with going looking for it, as if that might be a way to earn more merit, or get to heaven faster. I can't think of a single story about St. Peter sitting at the pearly gates asking folks how much they've suffered.

So, what is Jesus talking about? "If any want to become my followers," he insists, "let them deny themselves and take up their cross and follow me." It begins in denying self. Where do we do that in our daily lives? Maybe we turn down an extra serving at dinner, or choose to keep driving our old car, or go to the gym. It's not so much a matter of choosing self-denial as it is choosing one good in place of another. There's nothing wrong with eating dessert, or buying a new car, or lounging on the couch. But it may be that today we need to choose the other, in hopes of something better. Athletes know a lot about self-denial—it's what training is all about. None of us makes those kinds of decisions perfectly, but learning to make them is a big part of growing up. We spend a lot of energy teaching children how to make them. When Jesus says, "Deny yourself," he's really talking about getting out of the instant self-gratification mode and making conscious decisions about how we spend the resources of our lives. Good stewardship, in other words.

Denying self is also about getting out of the center of our own attention, out of the place that rightfully belongs to God. It is about recognizing our place as creature, rather than creator.

"Deny yourself, and take up your cross, and follow me." What is the cross, most fundamentally? Make a verb of it. To cross, to intersect, to pass from one side to the other. What crosses or is crossed in that instrument of murder? Christians have from the very beginning understood that the cross marks a bridge from earth to heaven, from mortal to immortal, from the divine to the human—maybe that's the vertical part of the cross. The other direction has something to do with reaching out to all humanity and all creation. We often cite the cross as a place where "the whole world came within the reach of God's saving embrace." The cross is an act in which the divine becomes human, and the human divine, and the larger creation is embraced. Maybe an act in which we get out of ourselves, or our selfish interests. Where something dies in order that a larger life may be realized.

Take up your cross. Other gospels speak of doing it daily. Where in our lives do we find opportunities to become more than our usual selfish reactions? Maybe it's getting up in the middle of the night to tend to a hungry baby. Certainly the child learns something about love in that act, and about the reality of love in the human caregiver. That adult has crossed over from his or her own personal need for sleep to the need of another. When a decision like that is made, heaven comes on earth, the reign of God becomes real right here and right now. Sometimes those decisions are terrifying. Sometimes we make those decisions knowing full well that something is going to die, and it very well may be mortal flesh. The emergency workers of our communities make those decisions willingly every day—firefighters and police and peacekeeping troops—all have crossed into danger for the sake of others. Those are honored callings, and ones for which we don't always give adequate thanks.

Sometimes the decisions are terrifying in other ways. We're not asked to be fearless, however, but faithful. When the call to let my name be submitted for bishop of Nevada first came, I dismissed it—preposterous! But it came again. And again. The persistence was terrifying when I began to really think about it. Eventually I said yes. I didn't know if I was called to be bishop, but I was certain that I'd been called to be part of this process.

When we learn to look and listen, all of us can begin to find cross-shaped decisions confronting us. They may look deadly, or fearsome, or at first impossible. Those decisions are all around us. How we respond has a lot to do with who we believe Jesus is. That's how Mark 8:27 begins, with Jesus asking, "Who do people say that I am?" and then, "Who do you say that I am?" Is Jesus the judge to be feared? Is he brother, or lover? Is he one like us, continually faced with cross-shaped decisions? One who through those decisions brings heaven and earth into the same event and embraces all creation.

One small example. I heard it a long time ago—perhaps it is apocryphal, perhaps literally true. One Sunday morning a man came into a church that was pretty concerned with doing things "decently and in good order." He was a bit aromatic, pretty scruffy looking, with wild hair and no socks. He wandered up the aisle, looking for a place to sit, but the pews were full. He kept going, and finally came up to the very front, and sat down on the floor, right under the pulpit. Everybody else was anxiously looking around, trying to decide what would happen next. One of the ushers, a man in his eighties, most properly dressed in a three-piece suit, came slowly up the aisle. You could hear his cane tapping out every step— no carpet in that church! People began to relax, knowing that he would do what needed to be done. Finally the usher got to the front, set his cane down on the floor, and with great difficulty, lowered himself to the floor to sit next to the stranger, so he wouldn't be all alone up there in front.

All of us get cross-shaped opportunities every day. Fear is what usually keeps us from responding to those opportunities. We never walk alone through the valley of the shadow of death. Our brother has been there before us, and while the result then was glorious, the journey through that valley is still bringing new and more abundant life. Our job is to embrace those opportunities for abundant life. That is where true joy is to be found.

Calling All Saints

I was called by a nickname until well into adulthood. And then one day I ran across my baptismal certificate, and I discovered that I'd been named for St. Katherine of Vadstena, in Sweden. She is hardly a household name, and she's not on our Episcopal calendar of saints. I didn't know who she was, but I started looking. I never found great reams of information, but I did find out that her mother, Bridget—an intriguingly Irish name for the middle of Sweden—had founded a double monastery after she was widowed in the middle of the fourteenth century. Her daughter Katherine joined her in that monastery. Bridget was apparently something of a preacher and politician, and at some point began taking pilgrimages to Rome and to the Holy Land. Eventually she began to ask the popes to return to Rome from Avignon. Her daughter went with her and carried on her work after she died, and even went back to Rome to encourage the competing popes to stop fighting with each other. Katherine of Vadstena's feast day is two days before my own birthday, which I am sure is why my mother put her down on my baptismal certificate.

Learning some of this led me to decide to claim my full baptismal name. That saint inspired me to claim more of who I was invited to become when I was baptized at nineteen days of age.

That's probably one of the most important functions of saints—they're examples and models for the rest of us. Who would you claim as a holy hero? One of the ancients like Isaiah, or Mary or Martha? Somebody like Desmond Tutu or Mother Teresa? What have those saints shown you?

Those great saints are pretty obviously holy folk, but they are not always terribly recognizable in their own lifetimes. There are lots of silent and anonymous saints. Sometimes events conspire to make one of them well-known.

Rosa Parks was a quiet woman, with a very simple message, and she had a pretty strong claim on her own dignity. There were other African American people who sat down on seats in the white sections of buses in the 1950s, but she is the one who is remembered as an icon of the civil rights movement. She was very simply clear about how she understood the gospel—and she took a lot of heat for her claim to equal treatment. She got death threats, she lost her job, and before long she and her husband had to move out of Birmingham. Saints don't always have an easy road.

Who or what is a saint? They aren't just the great heroes of our faith. Every baptized person is a saint, each one of us called to holy living. As the hymn says, saints are just folk like you and me.

Some biblical readings put some flesh on that idea of being holy. Revelation talks about the great crowd of witnesses, those from every family, language, people, and nation, that is, everyone who worships God. The psalm speaks of those who fear God. Fearing God does not mean cowering in the corner in abject terror. It means something more like proper reverence and respect. That word "worship" is related—it comes from the same root as "worth" and "worthiness"—we respect and revere that which is worthy of our attention. Saints are those who love God.

Jesus' words about the blessed ones in the Beatitudes are about how a saint lives—the other half of the great commandment to love God and love our neighbors as ourselves. Those who can love a neighbor as themselves are people who have an appropriate sense of self-worth. We have to love ourselves before we can love anybody else. Blessed are the meek, for they know they aren't the center of the universe. It's got something to do with looking after other people too, not just my own infinite wants.

I heard a great story on the radio about a woman who claimed a new name as an adult. It's really about appropriate love of self and others. She'd been abused as a child and she took her mother's name when she turned eighteen. She went on to make a movie about all the other women in this country who share the name Angela Shelton. What she discovered says a lot about domestic violence and abuse, but also about survival and resurrection. Angela Shelton took her name, which she might have understood as something entirely unique, and used it to find a common experience with many, many others. She built community.

Blessed are the poor in spirit, for they know that the spirit is not their own creation. They understand themselves as creatures. They have an appropriate sense of humility—made of the earth yet also created in the image of God. Blessed are the merciful, who act out of a sense of the mercy of God. I think of a couple of lawyers I know who spend their lives trying to undo legal injustices—they work for the deliverance of prisoners who are innocent, who have gone to death row on flimsy evidence or on apparently racist charges. The man and the woman I bring to mind know themselves and the legal system as fallible, yet they continue to seek truth.

Blessed are those who mourn, who have loved well and deeply, and know that the healing they crave will not come by their own efforts. I know a woman whose much-beloved husband of more than thirty years died a few years ago. She is abundantly re-invested in life, yet she still bears scars from the loss of that deep and abiding love, and she will carry those scars to the grave. Yet those scars have only increased her sense of compassion for the people and the world around her.

Blessed are the saints who are pure in heart, who seek the image of God in the folks they meet. I know a fellow who's had an incredible streak of agony in the last few months. His supervisor at work is abusive, his daughter miscarried an early pregnancy in the midst of her own wedding, and he was attacked by pit bulls as he took an evening stroll in his own neighborhood. The dogs' owner took him to the emergency room and checked on him a couple of days later. Lots of folks would have been out for blood after a month like that, but he's taken all that sour luck and made lemonade. He is seeing the blessings in life rather than the string of griefs, and he's even managed to build a relationship with the owner of those dogs. Blessed are the persecuted, who know their dependence on God.

Saints are folks who share the dream of God for a society of shalom, a community of peace and justice. Those folk who hunger and thirst for righteousness, who seek peace, are the prophets of our age, the ones who proclaim the dream of God and work to make it reality. They are people like Nelson Mandela, and those of you who feed the hungry, and the legislators who care for the least and the lost and the left out in this land of ours.

Blessed are those who love God and who love their neighbors as themselves.

In our baptism, we were all invited to be saints, to love God abundantly, to respect the dignity of the God-bearers around us, and to help to build that dream of God's peace in this world. There's not any reason, no, not the least, why we shouldn't be saints too.

PART EIGHT

TAKING FLIGHT

Mission and Ministry

Why Exactly
Are We Here?

I can remember writing to my bishop when I was in seminary and musing on the challenge of learning to balance so many different demands, and how that must surely be good preparation for parish ministry. Little did I know that it had more to do with learning that ministry is really about responding gracefully to the interruptions.

Anselm of Canterbury knew a thing or two about ministry. He asserted that the Christian theological task was to continue to seek confirmation and understanding of the faith that is already within us. Most of us at some time or other probably think the basic Christian theological task is just the reverse to seek more and deeper understanding in order to shore up the flimsy belief we can't quite keep hold of.

After all, we don't get much reaffirmation of the reality that we are all beloved, even in the best seedbeds. There is often more manure and pruning than gentle rain and sweet talk for the seedlings. It helps to come here with a real confidence that one is truly beloved.

Isn't that what Jesus is getting at in that passage from Matthew? The things hidden from the wise and intelligent are more about the reality of being beloved, the actuality of grace, and that we are surrounded by God, that we can't ever run out of God, than they are about theological arcana or liturgical gnosis. You will spend a long time in the library before you discover the reality of knowing you are loved in the dusty pages of old theological tomes, but you will find deeper confirmation if that's what you're truly seeking.

Seminarians who leave home and family, former occupation, or old way of life to prepare for ministry can find themselves on an avenue to the riches of grace. But that grace comes in ways that will challenge the academic snob within the church. We are utterly beloved whatever we do,

whatever grade we get, no matter how we botch our sermons or flub liturgical singing. Our ultimate worth is based not on the fineness of our writing but on the fact of our being. I do not say that as one who disdains the
intellectual life. I have spent nearly thirty years of my life in one academy
or another. But all the wonders and marvels of that life cannot produce
belief or salvation, in ourselves or any other. None of us can be an effective
minister of good news until we know ourselves beloved.

There is a dying necessary before the seedlings can truly begin to
thrive in this or any seedbed. A dying to achievement for its own sake, a
dying to believing merit will bring salvation, a dying to assuming that
fancy thinking makes a great spiritual leader. A dying to believing that
grace is always soft and sweet and easy to take.

When I first met my husband, he was coming off fifteen years of high-
level mountain climbing. When I heard his stories, I too wanted to learn
how to dance up a rock face with a minimum of effort, and I took a course
in rock climbing at the local community college. Eventually Dick began to
share some of what he knew. Most of it had to do with attitude, and he
wouldn't ever have talked about it as spirituality, but it was. He talked
about learning how to practice pain—scuffed knuckles and sleeping cold
and eating what you had left in your pack at the end of a long trip
(remember that story about making a stew out of kippered herring and
coconut pudding?). Mostly it had to do with learning that the glorious
experience of transcendence that comes with living fully in the moment—
usually stretched out reaching for the next hold with a thousand feet of air
below you—only comes with a good dose of suffering because it takes
complete and utter, full and total commitment.

So does ministry.

This wonderful and awe-filled thing called ministry is a gift that's given
to us in the dying and rebirth of baptism. It brings with it opportunities to
learn vulnerability, to learn how to serve the world's insatiable needs, and
it brings opportunities to learn how to practice the dying that leads to resurrection. All ministers of the gospel have ample opportunities to practice
the pain of dying. Paul knew about practicing pain and the transcendent
opportunities that come with total commitment. And they're even more
glorious than a mountain wall.

God is to be found in the glories of the mountaintop just as much as
in the pain and peril of the pit. They're often the same. Trusting in the

love of God in the midst of it all is the only thing that's required—but not in the sense of having to do anything more than relaxing into it. Trust means exercising, training our eyes and ears and hearts to recognize that kind of surprising, wondrous, even seemingly foreign love in the best and the worst the world can dish out—expecting, insisting, demanding, beating on the door of heaven like the widow demanding justice of the crooked judge. "I know you're in there, God, so you'd better come out and show yourself!"

Practicing resurrection, as Nora Gallagher's lovely book puts it.

Practicing resurrection means learning to embrace the character-building and the interruptions that confront us at every turn, knowing as confidently as Anselm that deeper understanding lies around the next corner and in the next challenging encounter. And that always, always, always, that understanding is rooted in the seedbed of knowing ourselves utterly beloved. Wherever I go, there you are, O God, in the valley of the shadow of death, in the farthest depths of the sea, on the highest and most glorious mountain peak, and in the nadir of despair. And yet, O gracious one, I still hear your voice intoning, "You are my beloved. In you I am well pleased."

Stretched on the Frame
of the Holy Spirit

It's a provocative image, "being stretched on the frame of the Holy Spirit." The more I think about it, the more it seems to be a good metaphor for ministry.

What else do we stretch on frames? Canvas gets stretched so that it's solid enough to put oil paint on. Animal skins get stretched in order to start the curing and tanning process. Skins are stretched on another kind of frame to make a drum. When I was growing up, my mother used to put my dad's newly washed woolen socks on frames so they wouldn't shrink or pull out of shape. They make similar frames for woolen sweaters. Anybody who's ever done embroidery knows that having a frame helps in a lot of different ways. It makes the embroidery stand out from the background, it keeps the stitches even, and it makes a flimsy piece of cloth a lot easier to handle. Beading and weaving is far easier to do on the kind of frame we call a loom. All of these kinds of stretching limit mobility—they make a flexible surface inflexible or less flexible, in order to produce something that couldn't be produced otherwise. This kind of stretching uses tension productively, and what is produced may be a complete surprise. A limp piece of animal skin suddenly produces the wonderful booming sounds of a bass drum.

Sometimes the stretching can actually make the thing expand—think about some of the stranger kinds of surgical procedures. I read an article about twin boys joined at the head, who were getting close to two years old. In order to prepare them for separation, balloons were placed under their skin so it would stretch to cover the wounds when they were finally separated. Sometimes a similar thing is done to help bones grow or heal. A leg may be broken, for example, and set in a frame, and the edges of the frame forced apart a tiny distance more every week or so. The bone actually grows to fill the space, and so does the soft tissue.

So what might all this have to do with us, being stretched on the frame of the Holy Spirit? Living in tension, having the limits of a framework, expanding capacity, and growing—sound familiar? Sounds like ministry to me.

Think about the tension involved in the difference and opposites we all live with. The frame on which deacons are stretched—or hung out to dry, depending on your current experience—has one end in the world and the other in the midst of the worshiping community. There's supposed to be a tension between the two—because they have not yet been completely reconciled, and the reign of God has not been established everywhere. All of that tension means there is still work to do, and that's why at the end of every Eucharist we are sent out, to get busy doing that work.

Christians are meant to be stretched on a frame like that, a frame that unites heaven and earth. Isaiah reminds us that God may give us the bread of adversity and tears of affliction, but neither will God hide from us. Life will not always have such deep suffering, but it will have tension, and ambiguity, and paradox. God is present even in the midst of suffering, God is still working his purposes out, and we will be stretched between suffering and joy.

There's a lot of road imagery in the gospel. "I am the way," Jesus says. That road—sometimes called the narrow road—is a kind of frame. The edges of the road, the barriers that keep us from wandering off, are no different from the sides of the frame. They are the limits, either innate or chosen, that keep us going in the right direction. The Ten Commandments, the baptismal covenant, the vows that clergy take at ordination—all of them are guides to keep us moving toward that reign of God. Sure, they produce tension—there are times when most of us would find it easier to ignore the injustice in our own backyards—but those edges of the frame continue to draw our attention to what is going on in the orchards and sweatshops, to the way the least among us are being ignored or exploited.

There are a variety of frames in this life we call Christian. Some focus on the least and the lost and the left out, making us uncomfortable and producing some tension in us, so that more of us will join in that work of seeking the reign of God here and now.

When we choose one frame it limits other choices, but the tension that's produced can be enormously creative. Think about marriage, or the decision you have made to follow a particular vocation. Choosing to go through one doorway means other passages are no longer accessible. When I quit doing oceanography, I very soon became unemployable, because I wasn't current, I wasn't up on all the latest discoveries. But going through the chosen door opens many, many others. Being stretched on the frame of the Holy Spirit means letting go of some possibilities in favor of others that can be enormously productive. We accept the limitations, the guidelines, and we welcome that tension so that we can resonate like cowhide—boom, boom, boom. How could we possibly predict that a dead piece of cow could produce such a lively sound? If we're willing to be similarly stretched, we can become instruments that can convert spiritual energy into a changed society. And every once in a while we'll make sweet, sweet music.

Any one of us engaged in a spiritual journey, or Christian living, or baptismal ministry, knows what that stretching is like. All of us are asked to do a lot of stretching. A calling to the diaconate or the priesthood? Rebuilding the sanctuary? Feeding women and children leaving violent relationships?

The apostles Philip and James are among the least known—they are routinely confused with others who have the same name. They were not the big stars around Jesus. Philip is the one who says to Jesus, "Who, us? Feed all these five thousand people? No way!" And they all get stretched a bit more, and suddenly everybody is fed and then some.

The cross is probably the ultimate symbol of being stretched on a frame. Jesus is stretched between heaven and earth, uniting them and us in a frame that willingly lets no one go. Being stretched out also means there's nothing left to hide. Do you know that famous double image of a human being—one of Da Vinci's drawings—that shows a human being stretched out as if on a wheel? That's a vulnerable way to live. People can see you, warts and faults and sins and all. But it's also a gift, because it says that if I can stand to live this way then maybe you can, too.

Let yourself be stretched on a frame. Live and love in the tension between where you are and where the rest of the world is meant to be. And draw your neighbors into that tension, so that they, too, can be stretched into people with bigger hearts—hearts that don't just go thump, but resound with the booming love of God. It is not the size of the drum that matters, but the strength of its voice.

God, with Skin

A while back, I was sitting eating my lunch and reading a little magazine called *Outlook*. It's put out by a group in England that continues to campaign for the full inclusion of women in the ordained ministry of the Church of England; at the moment, women can serve as priests but not bishops. I found a wonderful poem there by June Wyton, who died in 2003. It was given to the first women in England as they were preparing for ordination as priests, in March 1994.

> The door is open and the women come
> Praising and singing, walking hand in hand
> Praising and singing we will welcome them
> And gather at the altars where they stand.
>
> November now shall be a month of joy
> Dawn after darkness, rainbow after rain
> The year will turn, the Christmas star will rise
> And Christ will be laid in women's hands again.[8]

Here in the United States it's been nearly thirty years since we began to see women at the altar and receive Christ from their hands, so perhaps it's hard to remember how poignant—or unsettling, or even shocking—that experience was. It is still true that most of the women clergy in our church did not grow up with a vision or understanding of a call to be priest—it was unheard of when they were little girls. That is changing. I have a friend in Oregon who tells a remarkable story about a young boy who is growing up on the coast. His church has a woman as a priest. When this little boy came to visit relatives in Portland, they took him to a church he'd never visited before. After the service, he exclaimed to his parents, "You mean boys can be priests, too?"

---

8. June Wyton, in *Outlook* (the publication of WATCH—Women and the Church) 15 (Autumn 2003). Used by permission.

Sometimes God calls unexpected people to unexpected ministries. None of us knows where we're going until we can say, "Here I am, send me." Even then, we don't know the end of the road, but we understand which road we're meant to travel.

The job of a priest is to equip the saints for ministry—to help and challenge us all to discern where God is calling us, to discover the gifts we have to answer that challenge, and to get out there and do something about it.

The role of priests is to be a visible reminder that ministry is about getting out of our own way—a reminder that "minus" and "ministry" have the same root. Like John the Baptist, the priest's job is to point to another. That's what Paul is trying to tell the folks in Thessalonika: "As you know, and as God is our witness, we never came with words of flattery or looking for money, nor did we come looking for praise." It's not our own message we're bringing; we are here to share the dream of God. And then Paul gets to the heart of it: "So deeply do we care for you that we are determined to share with you not only the gospel of God but also our own selves," he writes, "because you have become very dear to us." This kind of minister shares good news, but does it in his or her own self. Christ is laid in this person's hands (and yours and mine and yours and yours . . .). That's the only way most of us ever get to meet Christ—through the very human hands of someone with good news to share.

You know about the little girl whose mother had put her to bed only a few minutes before she appeared in the kitchen again. "Mommy, I'm scared." "No reason to be scared, you know God is with you." "But, Mommy, I want someone with skin on."

We are God with skin on, if we're willing to say, "Here I am, send me." But the God-part shows through that skin only if we let it, if we're open to being a clay vessel.

Probably the hardest task most of us ever learn is to be vulnerable with other people—especially people who may not understand or love us for ourselves—but they are part of that field ripe for harvest. Vulnerability is at the root of all good ministry. It starts with being open to an unexpected call and the immediate response: "Who, me?"

It proceeds to learning about our own unexpected gifts: "Yeah, right, call an introvert to preach!" And it continues in learning to be vulnerable to the needs and concerns of the folk around us. Jesus' vulnerability—

what we usually call his compassion—was a radical openness to everyone he met, and to their suffering. That included those social outcasts and the folks whom proper Jewish men should never have deigned to notice in public.

That's the harvest, those harassed and helpless crowds, the sheep without a shepherd. And as Pogo, a character from a popular 1940s comic strip, said, they is us. When we can acknowledge our own need, our own woundedness, vulnerability brings the possibility of intimacy with God. Connecting the two, vulnerability and intimacy with God, is priestly work. It is work that is often done in public, through teaching and preaching and gathering up all those wounds at the altar. And that work of bringing vulnerability into intimacy with God is work that every single one of us shares. The priest's job is to remind us that the work of compassion and reconciliation is baptismal ministry.

When a child on the playground reacts to a conflict with an attempt at mediation rather than violence, vulnerability moves toward intimacy, and the reconciling spirit of God is at work.

When someone wakes up to the human cost of many of the consumer goods we enjoy, and begins to question and lobby for change, God's dream begins to become real.

When we recognize our own deep hunger for relationship with something or someone beyond ourselves, we become human messengers and laborers in the harvest.

You and I have the ability to share the Christ laid in our hands. May we be profligate in sharing that gift, both good news and the help of our hands. May we bless all we meet with that gift of abundance, full measure, pressed down, and overflowing.

Human Candles

In Jewish tradition, the mother of a boy baby was expected to offer sacrifice in the Temple on the fortieth day after the child's birth. Mary would have offered those two pigeons or turtledoves as a sign of her re-entry into normal life after childbirth.

But this offering wasn't just about the mother. Every firstborn son in Israel was consecrated to God, in remembrance for what God had done in the Passover. Jesus was presented in the Temple, and his parents dedicated him to God.

In some parts of the church this feast is celebrated on February 2 as Candlemas. It's a feast of lights, much like Epiphany. Especially in England, there's a tradition of blessing all the candles to be used in the church in the coming year. It doesn't matter what kind of candles a parish uses—you could get out all the gallons of oil to be used this year, and offer a prayer of thanksgiving and dedication. You could get out little hand candles, like the ones we often use at the Easter vigil, and bless those. It would probably be even more appropriate to get out all the candles that will be given in baptism this year, with the words "receive the light of Christ," and bless those. Do you have a candle from your baptism? Do you ever get it out and light it? It's a wonderful tradition to start with children—light the candle on the anniversary of a child's baptism, and tell the story.

Ordination is something like that annual Candlemas blessing. You can think of it as blessing the ministry of a human candle, one of the baptized who are all called to be light to the nations. The ministry to which deacons and priests are called is and is not different from the ministry of any of the rest of us. If being baptized means that we are called to follow Jesus, then we too have been presented in a temple like this one, and asked to live like Jesus. In the beginning of John's gospel Jesus is called the light of all people, and then it goes on to say, "The light shines in the darkness, and the darkness did not overcome it." The light of the world brings hope in the darkest of all possible places, in the valley of the shadow of death, in despair, in destitution, in utter depression and final desperation. There is great need for the light of Christ in this world.

We're all meant to be live out there as beacons of hope, spreading light into the dark places. Deacons have a taste of what it means to encourage us in that work of lighting up the world. Perhaps we should call them "deacon beacons."

We don't have a clear historical record of the development of priesthood, but over time the church did begin to intuit that a priest had to be a deacon first. The ministries of a priest and deacon have a different focus, but they both have their roots in the promises we all make at baptism: will you respect the dignity of every human being? Will you strive for justice and peace among all people? Will you seek and serve Christ in all persons? Will you proclaim the good news of God in Christ both in word and example? Deacons have a special calling to servant ministry, to help and aid those on the margins—the forgotten and ignored of this world. Deacons are meant to pester the rest of us to notice those who have been forgotten in the dark places of this world, and then to do something about it. The particular priestly ministry of reconciliation has to be rooted in an awareness of people in need, and reconciling ministry makes no sense without it. Deacons are formed as images of servanthood, calling and urging and pushing and nagging the rest of us to do that kind of work in our own lives. They are candles for the rest of us.

When I think about candles, one of the first things that comes to mind is that old familiar poem by Edna St. Vincent Millay:

My candle burns at both ends
It will not last the night
But ah, my foes, and oh, my friends,
It gives a lovely light![9]

She is probably right that none of us candles will last the night—if we're burning alone. But when we come together, the light overcomes the darkness and dawn comes once more.

There's a wonderful Mexican art film from the late 50s entitled *Macario*. Macario is a poor wood-cutter whose name ironically means

---

9. Edna St. Vincent Millay, "First Fig," in *A Few Figs from Thistles* (New York: Harper & Brothers, 1922), 9.

"happy" or "blessed." He never has enough to eat, and his recurring dream is to have an entire roast turkey to himself. His wife spies a turkey in her rich neighbor's yard and smuggles it home and cooks it. She gives it to Macario early the next morning, and he hustles out into the woods to eat it in blessed solitude. But the aroma draws several people aside from their path, and they ask to share his turkey. One of his visitors turns out to be a divine messenger, who eventually shows him a great cave filled with candles. The messenger tells Macario that the candles are the lives of all humanity. Some are burning brightly, some seem almost ready to go out, but the darkness of that immense cave is dispelled by the steady light.

Light shines in the darkness, and the darkness does not overcome it. We too—all of us—are called by our baptism to shine forth like those candles in the cave. The ordained are also called to light other candles, to fan their flames, and to send those candles into the dark corners of this world.

In the English roots of our tradition, in the midst of the English Reformation, the various factions soon went to war with each other in an overwhelming spasm of darkness. Many good and holy examples lost their lives in the midst of those wars. There is an especially poignant story of two of the reformers, Nicholas Ridley and Hugh Latimer, who were burned at the stake in 1555. They are remembered for their conviction that every member of the church lives out the gospel in the dailiness of their lives—whether behind the plow or in the kitchen—and that paying attention to the needs of the poor is paramount in living the gospel. They are remarkable examples for the ministry of servanthood. The two are remembered as well for an exchange as they were led to the stake. In a wonderfully earnest and yet ironic charge, Latimer said to his friend, "Be of good comfort, Master Ridley, for we shall this day light such a candle by God's grace in England as shall never be put out."

Our servant leaders echo the hope of Jesus born as a humble child in a rude and darksome cave. Their ordination echoes Latimer's call to let the light burn so brightly the whole world will take courage and find reason to rejoice even unto death.

Works in Progress

In 2003 I went to Kenya to help dedicate a medical clinic that had been built in the Mua Hills, but even more to try to build a partnership with one or more of the dioceses in Kenya. It was a long way from the Diocese of Nevada, and the people I met in Kenya taught me a good deal about mission in another context.

The Diocese of Nevada is about half the size of the country of Kenya, with significantly fewer people—only about 2 million. There are thirty-seven congregations, and about five thousand Episcopalians—only about one percent of the size of the Anglican Church in Kenya. Nevada is mostly a desert—our annual rainfall is less than ten centimeters (four inches). There are many, many mountain ranges in Nevada, and very little agriculture, because there is so little water. In the last 150 years, the economy has primarily been based on mining—silver, gold, and copper—but in the last few decades tourism has come to dominate. Gambling has been legal in Nevada for more than fifty years, and there are many other, less savory diversions. There is much work for the church to do there.

The Diocese of Nevada has been a pioneer in the Episcopal Church for the last thirty years in developing creative ways to provide sacramental ministry in small and rural communities, and in encouraging a baptismal ecclesiology more closely aligned with the theology of our 1979 Book of Common Prayer. There are Episcopal churches in many of the small communities across the state. The church was planted in those communities when they were booming mining towns filled with people, and the church has stayed, even though most of the people have left. Most of those churches are more than a hundred years old, and their congregations are now very small—a handful to a few dozen people. We have learned how to ask those communities to look at their members to see who has the gifts of a deacon, a preacher, a priest, or a pastoral caregiver. Many of those congregations have called people to serve in those ministries, and they have been trained locally, and licensed or ordained to serve in those remote communities.

In the last twenty or thirty years a center of tourism in southern Nevada has grown like wildfire. At present, 75 percent of the people of Nevada live in Las Vegas, and it is the fastest growing city in the United States. We have a great opportunity to evangelize that rapidly growing population, and we need help to do so. Many people move to Las Vegas and Nevada from other parts of the United States and from around the world. One of our newest congregations is the African Christian Fellowship, founded and nurtured by a priest who came to us from the Diocese of Mt. Kenya South. Another new congregation in Las Vegas is composed of Filipino Christians.

The church in Nevada can learn something about evangelism and church planting from the experience of the Anglican Church of Kenya, and together we have begun to build partnerships that will bless both these parts of the Anglican Communion. That part of the body of Christ called the Anglican Communion just might be an opportunity for mission as well. The different parts of the Communion have not understood each other very well in recent years, and the Archbishop of Canterbury, Rowan Williams, has pointed to the reconciling work we share. In his enthronement sermon he said, "We have to learn to be human alongside all sorts of others, the ones whose company we don't greatly like, whom we didn't choose, because Jesus is drawing us together into his place, his company." He's talking about parts of the church that have been active opponents, but people who are strangers to each other have the same task of learning to be human alongside each other. Each part of the Body of Christ has enormous gifts—gifts which are different and not always understood, but gifts nonetheless. I went to Kenya to learn more about their abundant gifts, and to offer some gift from the Diocese of Nevada.

Let's look at mission even more broadly. What's the mission of the Church? Why have we been sent (for that is what "mission" means)? Why has each one of us been put on this earth? To restore all people to unity with God and each other in Christ. It doesn't just mean the different parts of the Anglican Communion, it means all God's children and indeed all of creation. God's mission for us is to build the reign of God. That's why we're here. And if we're not doing that, the master has come home and caught us sleeping on the job.

What is your mission? What has the master sent you to do? Mission comes in as many different forms as there are Christians. Your mission right now may be as a parent, or a teacher, or a medical worker, or a student, or a guitarist, or a copy editor. Our mission at election time is to vote for the candidates we believe will work to make a more just society. At this time in the world's history, all of us have a mission to work and pray for peace—in Iraq, in Israel and Palestine, in the Sudan—wherever there is strife or division in human society.

Our particular mission may change from year to year. During my time as an oceanographer, my mission was studying squids and octopuses in the north Pacific. I had heard that prayer after baptism that asks that the newly baptized may have "the gift of joy and wonder in all God's works." Studying those strange and wonderful sea creatures was my window into God's overflowing and outrageously abundant creativity.

And then my mission changed. When the opportunity to continue as an oceanographer ended, I was grief-stricken. But God is always at work, even when we can't quite see how. My priest helped me to wrestle with a call to the priesthood, and in God's own time, God sent me off to try a new way of building the reign of God.

If we're willing to pay attention, we can see that God is doing that kind of work all the time. God is continually asking us to wake up and pay attention to new ways of being missionaries. Where are you building the reign of God? What's your mission right now? How are you working to transform your family, or your work environment, or your community, into something more like the dream that God has for all of creation?

Mission is about how we live every day of the week. When we were baptized, we became missionaries—servants of the kingdom, builders of God's dream. When we dream that dream and do something about it, when we feed the hungry or clothe the naked or help a child resolve a schoolyard spat, we're being invited to the feast. Jesus says, "Come and share the banquet with my brothers and sisters, with my friends, with my poor and hungry and those on the margins." In serving them we are invited to sit down at the feast and meet Jesus, the master who serves, the king who puts on an apron and waits tables. Suddenly we discover that the guests of honor are those poor and hungry, but also those who serve them. This waiter-king has broken down all dividing walls. Everyone, absolutely everyone, is invited to the feast—all that's needed is to know hunger—your own or someone else's.

Remember what it is to be missionaries and dreamers of God's dream. Be alert, be ready, for the opportunities are all around us! There is Jesus, and here, and out there! Ho, you that hunger and thirst, turn in here, dream God's dream, join the feast at Jesus' table, keep inviting the guests. Ho, you that hunger and thirst, turn in here. We're going to keep on building this table bigger and bigger so that all the guests can join the feast.

Postscript

Homecoming

Where is home for you? How would you define your home? A friend in Nevada said to me just before I left that he had thought I would only leave Nevada to go home, and in his mind, that meant Oregon. But in the six years I spent there, Nevada became home. The state song is even called, "Home means Nevada." And for a place filled with folk who have come from elsewhere, that is quite remarkable—all sorts and conditions of rootless people trying to grow new roots in the desert.

So where is home for you? Des Moines or Anchorage or Taipei or San Salvador or Port au Prince?

What makes it home? Familiar landscape, a quality of life, or the presence of particular people?

Some people who engage this journey we call Christianity discover that home is found on the road, whether literally the restless travel that occupies some of us, or the *hodos*, or path, that is the Way of following the one we call the Christ. The home we ultimately seek is found in relationship with Creator, with Redeemer, with Spirit. When Augustine says "our hearts are restless until they find their rest in thee, O Lord," he means that our natural home is in God.

The great journey stories of the Hebrew Bible begin with leaving our home in Eden, they tell of wandering for a very long time in search of a new home in the land of promise, and they tell later of returning home from exile. And eventually Israel begins to realize that they are meant to build a home that will draw all the nations to Mount Zion. Isaiah's great vision of a thanksgiving feast on a mountain, to which the whole world is invited, is part of that initial discovery of a universal home-building mission, meant for all. Jesus' inauguration and incarnation of the heavenly banquet is about a home that does not depend on place, but on community gathered in the conscious presence of God.

In *Death of the Hired Man*, Robert Frost said that "home is the place where, when you go there, they have to take you in." We all ache for a community that will take us in, with all our warts and quirks and petty meannesses—and yet they still celebrate when they see us coming! That vision of homegoing and homecoming that underlies our deepest spiritual yearnings is also the job assignment each one of us gets in baptism—go home, and while you're at it, help to build a home for everyone else on earth. For none of us can truly find our rest in God until all of our brothers and sisters have also been welcomed home like the prodigal.

There's a wonderful Hebrew word for that vision and work—shalom. It doesn't just mean the sort of peace that comes when we're no longer at war. It's that rich and multihued vision of a world where no one goes hungry because everyone is invited to a seat at the groaning board, it's a vision of a world where no one is sick or in prison because all sorts of disease have been healed, it's a vision of a world where every human being has the capacity to use every good gift that God has given, it is a vision of a world where no one enjoys abundance at the expense of another, it's a vision of a world where all enjoy Sabbath rest in the conscious presence of God. Shalom means that all human beings live together as siblings, at peace with one another and with God, and in right relationship with all of the rest of creation. It is that vision of the lion lying down with the lamb and the small child playing over the den of the adder, where the specter of death no longer holds sway. It is that vision to which Jesus points when he says, "Today this scripture has been fulfilled in your hearing." To say "shalom" is to know our own place and to invite and affirm the place of all of the rest of creation, once more at home in God.

You and I have been invited into that ministry of global peacemaking that makes a place and affirms a welcome for all of God's creatures. But more than welcome, that ministry invites all to feast until they are filled with God's abundance. God has spoken that dream in our hearts— through the prophets, through the patriarchs and the mystics, in human flesh in Jesus, and in each one of us at baptism. All are welcome, all are fed, all are satisfied, all are healed of the wounds and lessenings that are part of the not-yet-ness of creation.

That homecoming of shalom is both destination and journey. We cannot embark on the journey without some vision of where we are going, even though we may not reach it this side of the grave. We are really charged with seeing every place and all places as home, and living in a way that makes that true for every other creature on the planet. None of us can be fully at home, at rest, enjoying shalom, unless all the world is as well. Shalom is the fruit of living that dream. We live in a day where there is a concrete possibility of making that dream reality for the most destitute, forgotten, and ignored of our fellow travelers—for the castaways, for those in peril or just barely afloat on life's restless sea.

This church has said that our larger vision will be framed and shaped in the coming years by the vision of shalom embedded in the Millennium Development Goals—a world where the hungry are fed, the ill are healed, the young educated, women and men treated equally, and where all have access to clean water and adequate sanitation, basic health care, and the promise of development that does not endanger the rest of creation. That vision of abundant life is achievable in our own day, but only with the passionate commitment of each and every one of us. It is God's vision of homecoming for all humanity.

The ability of any of us to enjoy shalom depends on the health of our neighbors. If some do not have the opportunity for health or wholeness, then none of us can enjoy true and perfect holiness. The writer of Ephesians implores us to maintain the unity of the Spirit in the bond of peace—to be at one in God's shalom. That is our baptismal task and hope, and unless each of the members of the body enjoys shalom we shall not live as one. That dream of God, that word of God spoken in each one of us at baptism, also speaks hope of its realization.

The health of our neighbors, in its broadest understanding, is the mission that God has given us. We cannot love God if we fail to love our neighbors into a more whole and holy state of life. If some in this church feel wounded by recent decisions, then our salvation, our health as a body is at some hazard, and it becomes the duty of all of us to seek healing and wholeness. As long as children live exposed on the streets, while seniors go without food to pay for life-sustaining drugs, wherever peoples are sickened by industrial waste, the body suffers, and none of us can say we have finally come home.

What keeps us from the tireless search for that vision of shalom? There are probably only two answers, and they are connected—apathy and fear. One is the unwillingness to acknowledge the pain of other people, the other is an unwillingness to acknowledge that pain with enough courage to act. The cure for each is a deep and abiding hope. If God in Jesus has made captivity captive, has taken fear hostage, it is for the liberation and flourishing of hope.

Augustine said that as Christians, we are prisoners of hope—a ridiculously assertive hope, a hope that unflinchingly assails the doors of heaven, a hope that will not cease until that dream of God has swallowed up death forever, a hope that has the audacity to join Jesus in saying, "Today this scripture has been fulfilled in your hearing."

And how shall that scripture be fulfilled in our hearing? In the will to make peace with one who disdains our theological position—for his has merit, too, as the fruit of faithfulness. In the courage to challenge our legislators to make poverty history, to fund AIDS work in Africa, and the distribution of anti-malarial mosquito nets, and primary schools where all children are welcomed. In the will to look within our own hearts and confront the shadows that darken the dream that God has planted there.

That scripture is fulfilled each time we reach beyond our narrow self-interest to call another home.

That scripture is fulfilled in ways both small and large, in acts of individuals and of nations, whenever we seek the good of the other, for our own good and final homecoming is wrapped up in that.

God has spoken that dream in us, let us rejoice! Let us join the raucous throngs in creation, the sea creatures and the geological features who leap for joy at the vision of all creation restored, restored to proper relationship, to all creation come home at last. May that scripture be fulfilled in our hearing and in our doing.

Shalom, chaverim, shalom, my friends, shalom.

> November 4, 2006
> National Cathedral of Saints Peter and Paul
> Washington, D.C.

Saints on Fire

I read a fascinating editorial last weekend anticipating All Saints' Day—and in a secular newspaper, no less! The Roman Catholic Church is apparently considering sainthood for a man who was executed in 1957. Jacques Fesch was accused, found guilty, and eventually guillotined for killing a police officer in the course of a robbery three years earlier. A year after his conviction, while he was in prison, he underwent a profound conversion that began a season of radical amendment to his life. He spoke of his experience by saying, "The spirit of the Lord seized me by the throat." The archbishop of Paris began the canonization process twenty years ago, and there is some hope that one day this man will be named a saint.

Saints—the holy ones, the elect, the baptized, the heroes of our faith—they are understood in a variety of ways. Basil the Great said about them in the fourth century: "The Spirit is the dwelling place of the saints, and the Saints are a place for the Spirit to dwell, as in a home, since they offer themselves as a dwelling place for God and are called God's temple."

We might say that saints are those who find a home "on the way," in the course of following Jesus. And sometimes the encounter is very much like being seized by the throat. It must have seemed that way to Lazarus, and probably to the people standing around as he emerged from the tomb: "Unbind him, and let him go!" Jesus' own experience was no less shocking, even though the words in translation seem a bit tame: Jesus was deeply moved. He was greatly disturbed. He began to weep. In the Greek it says something more like he was "gut-wrenched." Jesus was in breath-stopping agony at the death of his friend and the grief of his sisters.

Saints are those who are vulnerable to the gut-wrenching pain of this world. Some of us have to be seized by the throat or thrown into the tomb before we can begin to find that depth of compassion. And perhaps unless we are, we won't leave our comfortable narrow lives—or our remarkably nasty ones—to wake up and begin to answer that pain.

In the early Church, baptism was meant to be that kind of life-altering encounter. New saints spent three years in the readying, and then were taken in the dead of night into the crypt, stripped naked, and drowned— only to emerge filled with new breath, doused with sweet-smelling oil, and given a new white robe. What you and I do on Sunday mornings today sometimes seems a pale imitation, yet it can have every bit the same effect. Two weeks ago I met a forty-something man I baptized and confirmed two years ago, whose life has taken a remarkable turn—from ordinary daily dullness toward meaning and deep compassion and an awareness of God in every part of his life, and the willingness to change his community into something that looks a good deal more like the dream of God.

When we remember our baptisms in the sprinkling during the Eucharist, most of us probably cringe. We don't like to get wet. But I hope and pray that you and I can welcome those surprising drops as a tiny reminder of what is meant to happen to us, over and over again, day after day after day. Die to the old, be unbound, come out into abundant life in service to the world. Wake up, and notice the suffering around us.

It is the willingness to experience that pain which more than anything else marks us as saints. The pain of the whole world—those who agree with us and those who might be called enemies. The pain of creation, abused for our pleasure. The pain of a six-year-old child in Ghana, sold into slavery, to bail a fishing canoe and repair nets for 100 hours a week so that his parents might eat.

When Wisdom insists that souls of the righteous are at peace, it can only be in a world where those divisions and evils are ended. It is a dream of shalom, when all peoples and all creatures have come home at last. But it is also a dream that can be at least partially realized in our own day. Whenever two children make peace on the playground, the saints can rejoice. Whenever two or three fish-slaves are set free, shalom abounds. The hope of the saints is without bounds, for it insists that shalom is possible in this life, and not only at the end of all things.

There is a fascinating line in the midst of that Wisdom reading that says, "In the time of their visitation they will shine forth and run like sparks through the stubble."

In the time of their visitation—is this the visit of God among the righteous? Or is it an occasion when the saints show up? The word that's translated as visitation might also be translated oversight, or realm of service. In Greek, it is *episkopeis*. When the saints turn up, or when the Spirit makes a home in the saints, then the saints begin to burn and set the world alight. Their oversight, their ministry, their ability to see and influence and pastor the world, is set afire. All the saints are meant to run like sparks through the stubble, through that dead and no longer fruitful stuff, the dross of this world. You and I are supposed to get lit and set that flame to burning by our willingness to be vulnerable to the suffering around us.

In western Oregon for decades the usual way to clean up the fields after a crop of grass seed was harvested was to set the stubble afire. Clouds of noxious smoke filled the skies, and often drifted for dozens of miles. Air quality issues have led to other ways of controlling the smoke output, but burning is still the very best way to sanitize the fields and get rid of the stubble. What do you think? Can we make holy smoke?

The *episkopeis* of the saints, their ministry, cleans the fields of that which cannot survive in God's dream of shalom, it burns away whatever limits that dream or cannot contribute to it. The ministry of governance, whether in the legislature, the polling booth, or in raising a child, is meant to prepare the ground for a new and abundant crop of life. Most of us here this morning will have an opportunity to exercise that kind of ministry on Tuesday. Will you consider your vote as an act of "running through the stubble"? Would that we might all be able to answer, "I will, with God's help."

Let the pain of this world seize us by the throat. Listen for Jesus calling us all out of our tombs of despair and apathy. May the shock of baptismal dying once more set us afire. This place we call home is meant to be a new heaven, a new earth, a holy city, a new Jerusalem. It is the sparks in the stubble that will make it so.

Turn inward for a moment and greet the spirit planted within you. When we come to the peace, turn to your neighbors and greet the saints, the fire-lighters in this field. Welcome, saint! Burn brightly and transform this world into God's field for life, full measure, pressed down and overflowing, meant for all humanity and all creation. Burn!

National Cathedral of Saints Peter and Paul
Washington, D.C.
November 5, 2006